AF291441

KAYODE OJO

EDEN

CLARION

KAYODE OJO

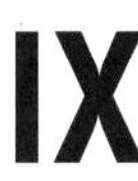

IX

Contents

Curator's Note: Shine Bright like a Diamond
Ebony L. Haynes

Steps from 52 Walker is the bustling intersection of Broadway and Canal, where the sidewalks are lined with knockoff designer bags and tourists and passersby enticed by the promise of owning a piece of perceived luxury at a fraction of the cost. This juxtaposition of high fashion and counterfeit goods sets the stage for Kayode Ojo's exhibition—an exploration of the thin line between the real and the replicated, the coveted and the commodified. Featuring flutes and handcuffs, chandeliers and gowns, *EDEN* epitomizes Ojo's knack for recontextualizing objects, imbuing them with new meanings and associations.

For the ninth exhibition at 52 Walker, Ojo transformed the gallery into a sanctuary that sat somewhere between the comfort of home and the allure of a party, creating a fleeting escape from the everyday. Throughout the run of the show, Ojo spent time in the space, calling it "church," a tongue-in-cheek nod to his upbringing and the idea that a church should be adorned with beauty in a visual expression of the congregation's devotion. The exhibition's title, *EDEN*, hints at a utopian space, here defined in terms of beauty, access, and luxury, while simultaneously touching on the impermanence and fragility of the ideal. As Ojo and I discussed while working on the show, in the book of Genesis, the story of Eden fits on a single page and yet holds so much reverence within society's understanding of such totemic dichotomies: right and wrong, good and evil, crime and punishment. Through the exhibition, Ojo connects this fleeting moment of biblical perfection with the historical and social struggles of the black middle class.

Ojo's work goes beyond mere aesthetic appeal; it questions our habits around consumption and the value we place on the commodities we acquire or desire. To make his sculptures, Ojo delves into his personal archives, transforming readymade items of leisure, luxury, and revelry into sleek, thought-provoking sculptures that straddle the line between delicate minimalism and glittering opulence. He sources his materials from eBay, Zara, and other online shopping hubs, occasionally inserting designer pieces among the knockoffs (without distinguishing the real from the fake), weaving the familiar rhythms of searching, scrolling, purchasing, and receiving into his artistic practice. Ojo deliberately seeks out objects that seem larger than life, things that crystallize our cultural fixations or aspire to an iconic status far beyond their fast-fashion origins. Once his purchases arrive in the studio, there are moments of discovery: Does the object match its online description? Is it of good quality? Does someone really need a birdcage of this size? Ojo then meticulously catalogues each item, reproducing its original online description in the medium line for his sculptures. These lists of overlapping search-optimized keywords probe the underlying algorithms of e-commerce.

In this volume of *Clarion*, Serubiri Moses situates Ojo's sculptures within the context of art and commerce through the lenses of consumerism, fetish, and queer culture. Moses's insights provide a critical framework to complement the visual experience of the exhibition. Emerging from the sensory overload of sequins, chrome finishes, and reflective surfaces, Ojo's sculptures seem almost self-aware, as if they know just how captivating their shimmering curves and edges are—tempting us back to the addictive, endless scroll of online shopping, where we'll see the haute couture designs presented during Fashion Week on zara.com, look at the Alaïa knockoff, and ask, "Who is she?"

Toward a Queer Postminimalism
Serubiri Moses

The Task of the Collector

The relationship between art and commerce is clear: art is sold in galleries, which operate within the art market, which is made up mainly of dealers, artists, collectors, and curators. Even art that interrogates commerce—including Kayode Ojo's—circulates in this sphere. This contradiction brings about the challenge of categorizing artworks as objects rather than as inquiries with their own context. The looping nature of art's relationship to commerce and then to inquiry mirrors Karl Marx's commentary on hoarding, which he calls a "Sisyphean task," one that is "boundless in its nature."[1] In other words, the collector of objects (whether garments or artworks or materials with which to make art) has no end in sight.

According to Marx, the logic of hoarding concerns money and its value, and it rests on the concept that "value is inseparable from the value-form."[2] This means that the object (value) itself can become a fetish or a commodity (value form). The intersection of fashion and art, as well as e-commerce and the art business, points back directly to the idea of hoarding. In the past decade, the exploitative nature of the fashion industry has been widely publicized. Garment workers, often in non-Western countries, are subjected to a practice akin to modern slavery through inhumane working hours driven by the overconsumption of fast fashion.[3] And yet the Western public continues to accumulate new clothing in excess, only to discard it when storage runs out or T-shirts rip, thereby making room for continued accumulation.

Building on these concerns, Ojo's process involves scouring e-commerce sites for items that affect luxury, purchasing and then storing, wearing, or otherwise using them, and eventually drawing on this object archive to make and remake conceptual sculptures. His work critiques overconsumption, especially within the realm of fashion but also within the commercial art world itself. Ojo describes overconsumption in the fashion market through the lens of fetish. As he has noted, "A lot of the clothing I use in my work is fast fashion or e-commerce. I like to complicate the hierarchy of real and fake."[4] By inhabiting the role of the collector—in this case, of knockoff garments and accessories—Ojo himself undergoes a process of hoarding. He admits, "I think sometimes it must actually be the fetish of spending money that makes people buy these things."[5]

The Fetish of the Object

Originally a reference to the fetish priests of West Africa, where fetish objects were the focus of magical and spiritual ritual, the term "fetish" has come to describe an object worship, excessive devotion, or sexual desire. Marx connected fetish to consumption when he wrote that the hoarder "sacrifices the lusts of his flesh to the fetish of gold. He takes the gospel of abstinence very seriously."[6] This allusion to sexual gratification gives some weight to Ojo's idea that the purchase of luxury goods can be merely gratuitous and shows us that the spending of money can be associated with object worship and desire.

If the fetish of object worship Marx describes can indeed be understood within the context of the art market, it is also important to consider that the art market consists not merely of galleries, artists, dealers, and patrons but also a whole range of other activities that are not the exclusive domain of financial exchange. Thus, within the context of Ojo's art (and its interrogation of commerce), the idea of commodity and fetish extends far beyond the object itself. According to Ojo, "the logic of my work is about evidence, a trace of something that's happened. I put on everything at least once before I use it in a sculpture."[7] Ojo's process of making conceptual sculpture relies on the acquisition and wearing of the luxury goods prior to (and sometimes again after) placing them in a gallery.[8] This is what I conceptualize as a process of resignification.

The term is borrowed from poststructuralism, where "resignification" is used to imply the way new meanings can be produced once symbols in a Cartesian field are reordered. I use "resignification" to refer to the reordering of contexts and meanings as exhibited objects travel from e-commerce sites to the artist's storage space, the artist's body, and the gallery space. Applied to the objects in *EDEN*, at 52 Walker, resignification brings to mind the way in which order and meaning are produced through the artist's appropriation and arrangement of objects. Here, I am referring to the ways luxury goods are displayed, such as the the two groups of chandeliers and the stack of champagne glasses (bought from CB2).

The artist's work is resignified through the dialectic of visibility and invisibility that becomes operative in *EDEN*. Implicating the viewer in the act of looking—and in the process of meaning-making—is another function of resignification. Without the viewer, and without the gallery space, Ojo's work is only partial, because it depends so strongly on the notion of the display itself, an approach the artist borrows from minimalist sculpture. The viewer's presence enables the artist to perform resignification, through which the work is truly assembled, and where it gathers meaning. Take, for example, the silver sequin gowns displayed on music stands, which recall the silver dresses worn by the actors Sarah Paulson, Tracee Ellis Ross, and Jaime King on the red carpet at the Emmy Awards in 2017[9] (the same year Ojo draped another silver dress over a couch in the group exhibition *Invisible Man*). Perhaps those seeing shiny sequin dresses in 2017 made an immediate association with these actors. In 2023, this viewer could think only of Beyoncé Knowles-Carter's floor-length silver Versace gown at the *Renaissance* movie premiere.[10] The viewer partakes in the meaning-making process, as intended by the artist.

Because the contexts of resignification in Ojo's work go beyond art, one can describe them as "queer." We understand queer theory to "challenge sexual, gender, class, and racial norms, and thus present a view of the binary order as culturally imposed rather than as natural law."[11] In Ojo's solo exhibition *Equilibrium* at Martos Gallery, we saw works such as *Closed Edition: Balenciaga Bootcut* (2018), a photographic print depicting the artist facing away from the camera, wearing only a flowing wig and bootcut Balenciaga jeans. Similarly, the silver sequin gowns in *EDEN* were, according

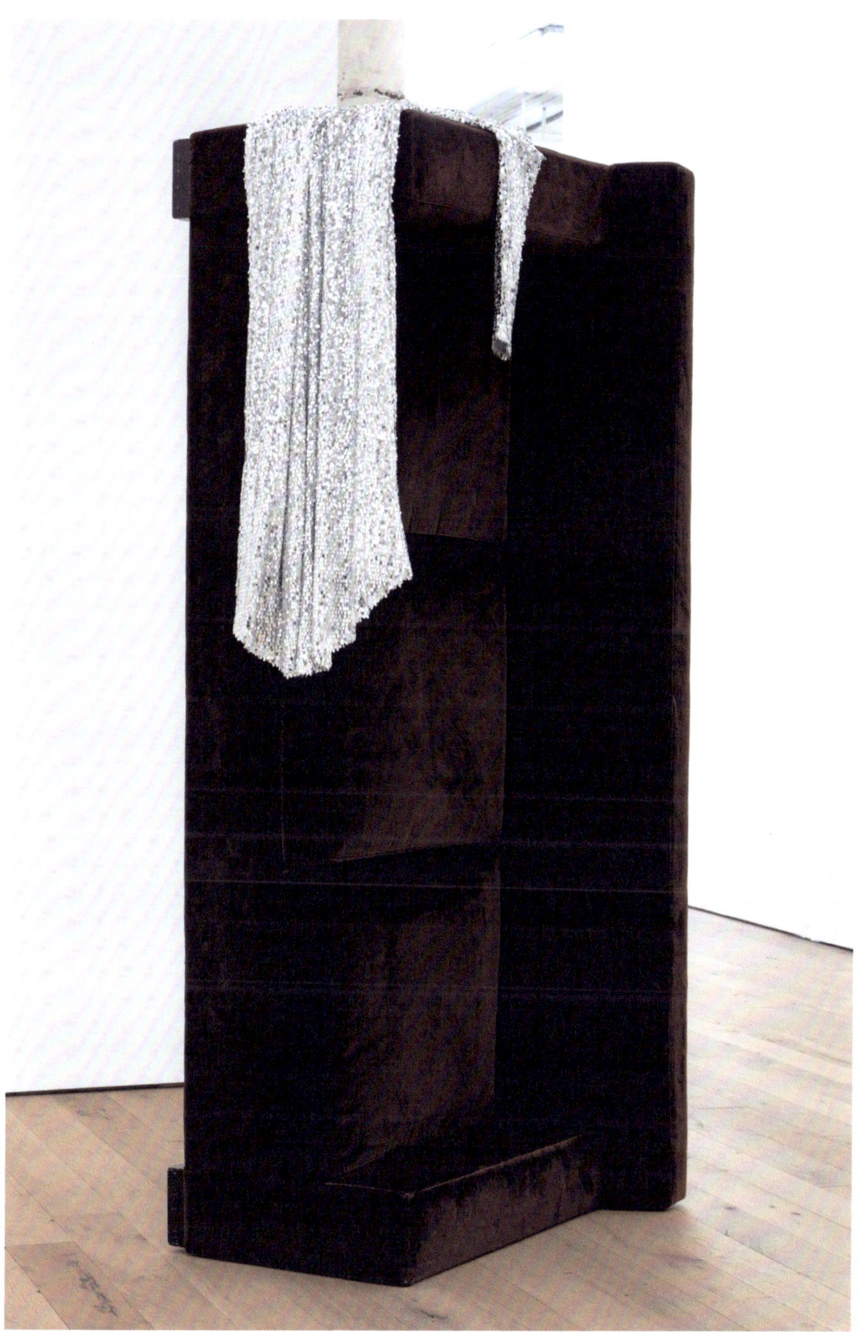

Untitled, 2017. Dark chocolate ABC Home sofa / couch; women silver sequins
long sleeves formal evening prom maxi cocktail party dress
90 × 40 × 30 inches | 228.6 × 101.6 × 76.2 cm

to Ojo, worn by him at least once prior to their display in the exhibition. These garments, designed for women and worn by a masculine-presenting artist, point to Ojo's work with nonnormative gender expression and queerness. The destabilization of categories of gender, race, and sexuality is present in the critical praxis of resignification.

Signifying Queen

In queer black and Latinx communities, "signifying" refers to the ways in which unique knowledge, language, and forms of communication are developed, shared, and circulated within the group. In 1991, the filmmaker Marlon Riggs used the term "signify" to address the simultaneity of the increased visibility of black and queer expression in popular culture and the invisibility of black queer people, as well as their negation in the hierarchy of black masculinity. Fashion here is synonymous with commodity and its (over)consumption—in this case, the absorption of black queer culture into the mainstream. Riggs used as an example Madonna, who visited New York's drag balls to recruit Latinx, black, and queer dancers for her Blond Ambition World Tour of 1990, and the subsequent widespread popularity of voguing—formerly a language of visual and bodily movement among queer black and Latinx communities. And yet, "Black Gay Man is a triple negation," Riggs wrote. "I am consigned, by these tenets, to remain a Negro Faggot."[12] Though the term "signify" typically refers to a form of expression, Riggs plays on its double meaning to pose a carefully formulated question to the queer black community at the periphery of the mainstream: "In a community where the dozens, signifying, dis'ing [*sic*], and *dishing* are revered as art forms, I ask myself: What does this obsession with Negro Faggotry signify? What is its significance?"[13]

This is reminiscent of the dialectic of visibility and invisibility of the resignified, and the unstable categories that constitute gender, race, and sexuality. When looking at the various objects Ojo uses in his conceptual sculpture, including the silver sequined gowns, that resignification constitutes

a kind of dissing, or "signifying" (to borrow Riggs's definition). Martos Gallery's 2017 group show *Invisible Man*, curated by Ebony L. Haynes and named for Ralph Ellison's 1952 novel, featured work that, according to Haynes, executed "an idea that I had of representing an absent body . . . and [spoke] to the lack of visibility of artists of color in the gallery space."[14] In the exhibition, Ojo showed *Untitled* (2017; p. 11), which features a sequined gown draped over a large brown velvet couch on its side. According to Haynes, "You can't sit on it. But someone has left their mark, giving the sense that it is no longer being used but not quite thrown away."[15] The feeling is of absence, and haunting. As Ellison notes on the very first page of *Invisible Man*: "No, I am not a spook like those who haunted Edgar Allan Poe.... I am invisible, understand, simply because people refuse to see me."[16] The implication of "ghost" here is one that can be understood within the realm of representation. In Ellison's terms it means that others have refused to acknowledge your presence and give reciprocity. Placed in dialogue with Ellison's novel, Ojo's work reveals the ways that such visibility is denied by the institutional structure of the art market and art museum and points to the erasure of artists of color from the mainstream.

Toward a Queer Postminimalism

There is something fascinating about the human and domestic scale at which Ojo makes his work. The writer Antwaun Sargent says Ojo's work "implicates the body in domestic space."[17] This relationship is suggested by the large brown velvet sofa in the *Invisible Man* exhibition and the room-length brown velvet curtain in *EDEN*. Though physically absent, the body is implicitly present everywhere in Ojo's work, an important way of marking the artist's queer, if not odd and unstable, relationship to minimalism.

The language of minimalism is related to the object's proximity to the body, as well as to the general use of gallery space as a medium. However, even more notably, minimalist vocabulary foregrounds both the body's absence and its presence. According to the curator Kynaston McShine, minimalist sculpture at times "intrudes aggressively on the spectator's space, or the spectator is drawn into sculptural space. Often the structure acts ambiguously, creating a spatial dislocation for the spectator with complex meanings."[18] Assembled from small household objects, Ojo's conceptual structures fit easily in the domestic space, "signifying" differently in their (sassy, femme) expression from the monumental sculpture of Richard Serra, Barnett Newman, Mark di Suvero, and Robert Morris, which expands outward and into the (masculine-coded) domain of architecture. This domestic scale ultimately provides for an unstable minimalist category and recalls the work of women sculptors in the minimalist tradition, such as Lynda Benglis and Eva Hesse.

The art historian David Getsy has called the sculpture of Dan Flavin and Constantin Brâncusi transgender.[19] I will at least provide that Ojo's conceptual sculpture unsettles the stable meanings of his materials, thereby "queering" them. The artist's own resignification of luxury goods into the gallery space both reorders their meanings and fetishizes them, implicating viewers in his meaning-making and his critique of commodity and overconsumption. From the perspective of queer theory, and its aim of challenging gender, class, and sexual norms, Ojo's work and exhibitions provide a queer rearticulation of minimalist vocabulary.

Notes

1 Karl Marx, *Capital*, vol. I (New York: Penguin, 1976), pp. 230–234.

2 Marx, *Capital*, pp. 130–134.

3 For more information, see "Working Hours and Overtime: 96-Hour Workweeks," Clean Clothes Campaign, https://cleanclothes.org/issues/working-hours.

4 Rafael de Cárdenas, "Artist Kayode Ojo on Class, Fakes, and Aspirational Glamour," *PIN–UP* 27 (Fall Winter 2019/2020).

5 De Cárdenas, "Artist Kayode Ojo on Class, Fakes, and Aspirational Glamour."

6 Marx, *Capital*, pp. 230–234.

7 De Cárdenas, "Artist Kayode Ojo on Class, Fakes, and Aspirational Glamour."

8 Kayode Ojo, in conversation with the author, January 4, 2024.

9 Erika Harwood, "Shiny Silver Gowns Dominate the Emmy Red Carpet," *Vanity Fair*, September 18, 2017, https://vanityfair.com/style/photos/2017/09/emmys-2017-silver-red-carpet-trend.

10 Kaitlin Clapinski, "Beyoncé Serves Galactic Glamour at the *Renaissance* Movie Premier," *Marie Claire*, November 27, 2023, https://marieclaire.com/fashion/beyonce-silver-versace-dress-renaissance-premiere.

11 Serubiri Moses, "It Shall Not Be Named—Carlos Motta: Your Monsters, Our Idols," *Art Papers* 46, no. 2 (Winter 2022/2023), p. 38.

12 Marlon T. Riggs, "Black Macho Revisited: Reflections of a Snap! Queen," *Black American Literature Forum: Black Film Issue* 25, no. 2 (Summer 1991), pp. 389–394.

13 Riggs, "Black Macho Revisited," pp. 389–394.

14 *Invisible Man* press release, Martos Gallery, 2017, https://martosgallery.com/exhibitions/49-invisible-man-torkwase-dyson-kayode-ojo-pope.l/press_release_text/.

15 *Invisible Man* press release.

16 Ralph Ellison, *Invisible Man* (New York: Vintage, 1989), p. 3.

17 Antwaun Sargent, "'Invisible Man' Inspires Conceptual Art About Blackness," *VICE*, July 21, 2017, https://vice.com/en/article/ev4wwm/invisible-man-inspires-conceptual-art-blackness.

18 Kynaston McShine, "Introduction," in *Primary Structures: Recent American and British Sculptors*. Exh. cat. (New York: Jewish Museum, 1966), n.p.

19 David J. Getsy, "Dan Flavin's Dedications," in *Abstract Bodies: Sixties Sculpture in the Expanded Field of Gender* (New Haven: Yale University Press, 2015), p. 209.

PLATES

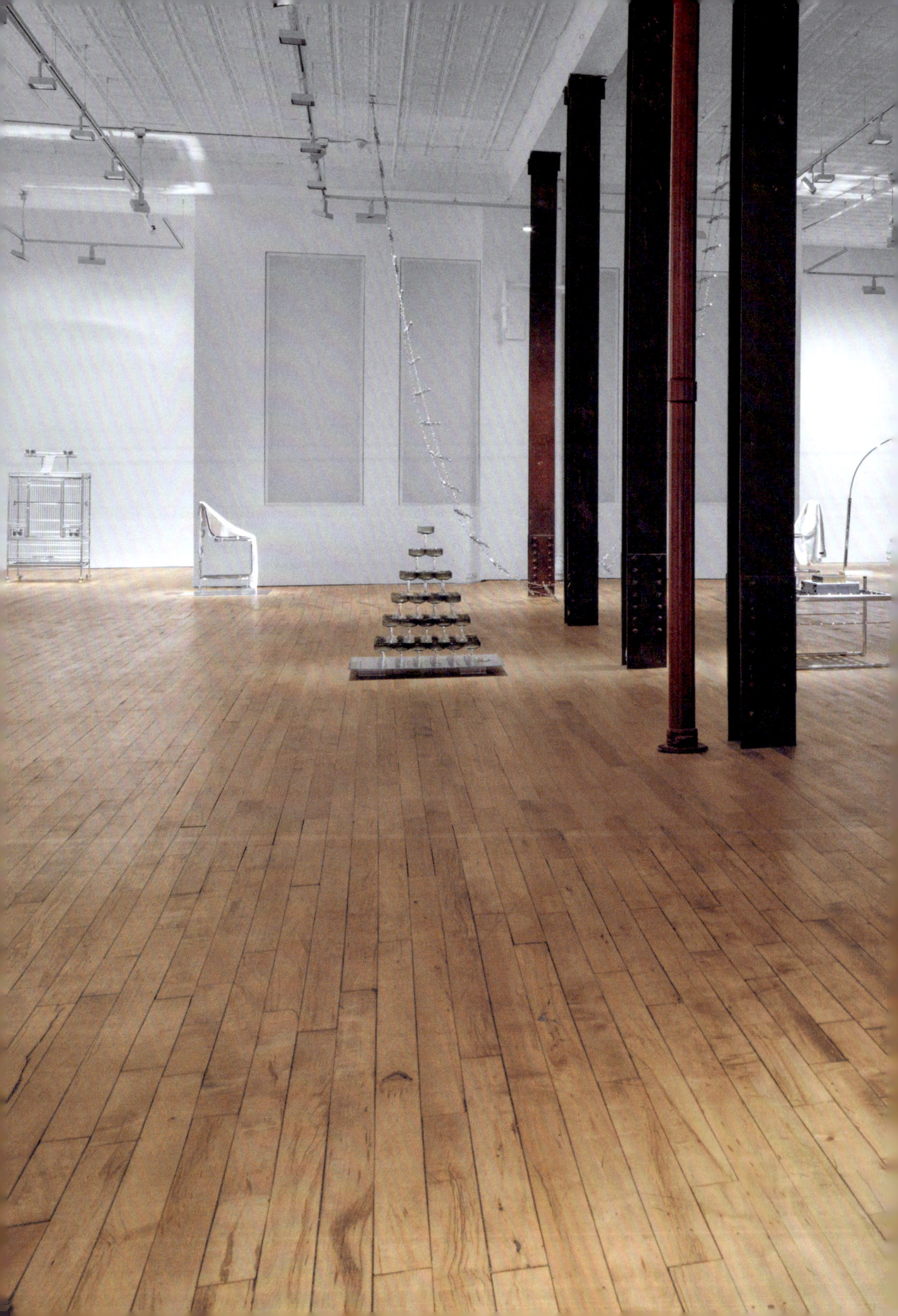

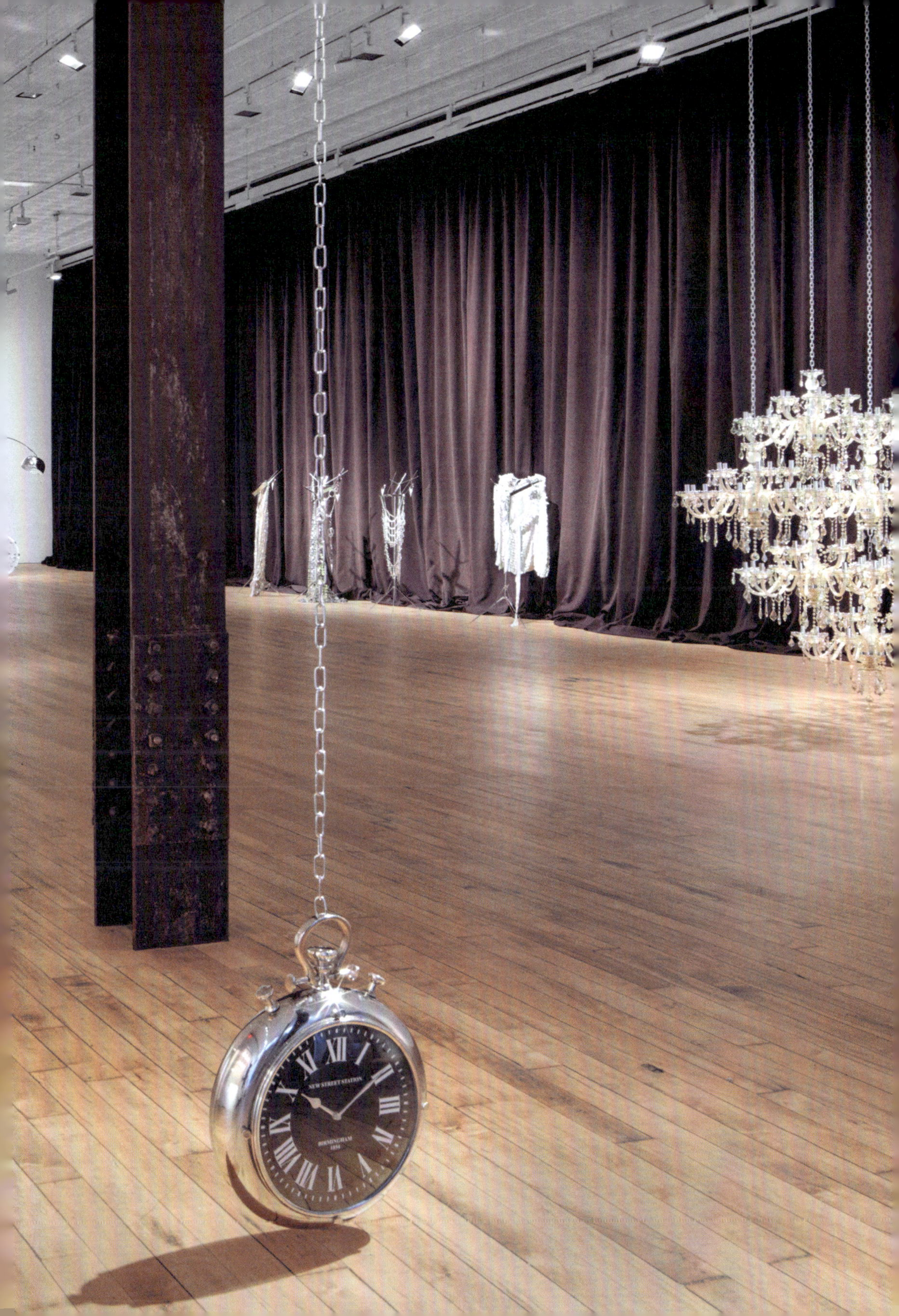

and the Pendulum, 2023
Deco 79 Stainless Steel Pocket watch Style Wall Clock, 16" x 6" x 22",
Silver; chandelier chain
16 × 14½ × 4½ inches | 40.6 × 36.8 × 11.4 cm

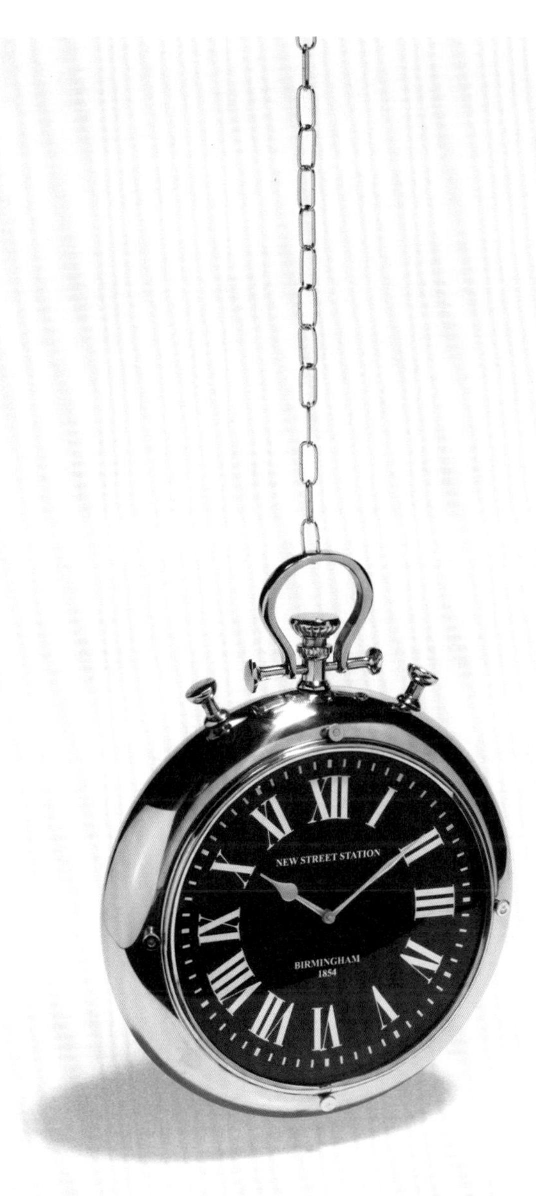
NEW STREET STATION
BIRMINGHAM
1854

Esther, 2023
Durahonn Luxury K9 Crystal Chandelier 15 Light, Modern Cognac Crystal Ceiling
Chandelier Lighting Fixture Candle Style E12 Base for Dinning Living Room
Bedroom Hallway (15 Lights)
72 ½ × 96 × 31 inches | 184.2 × 243.8 × 78.7 cm

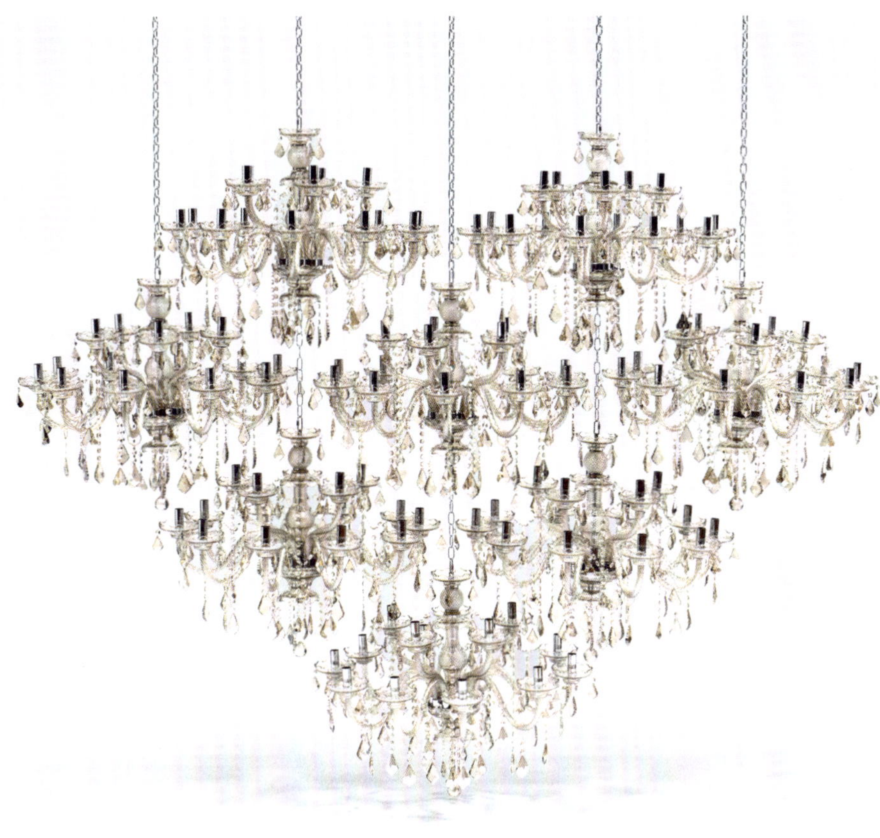

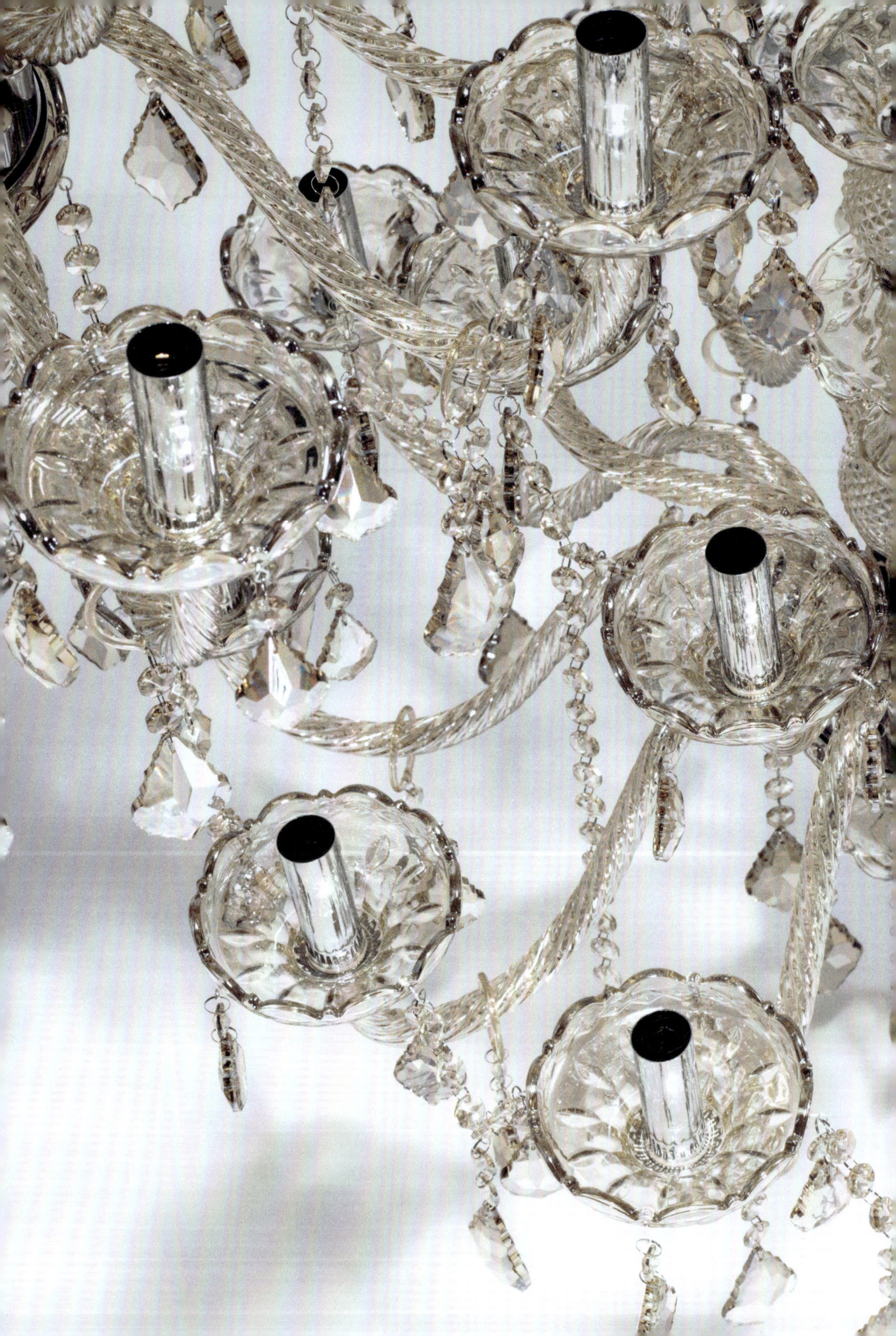

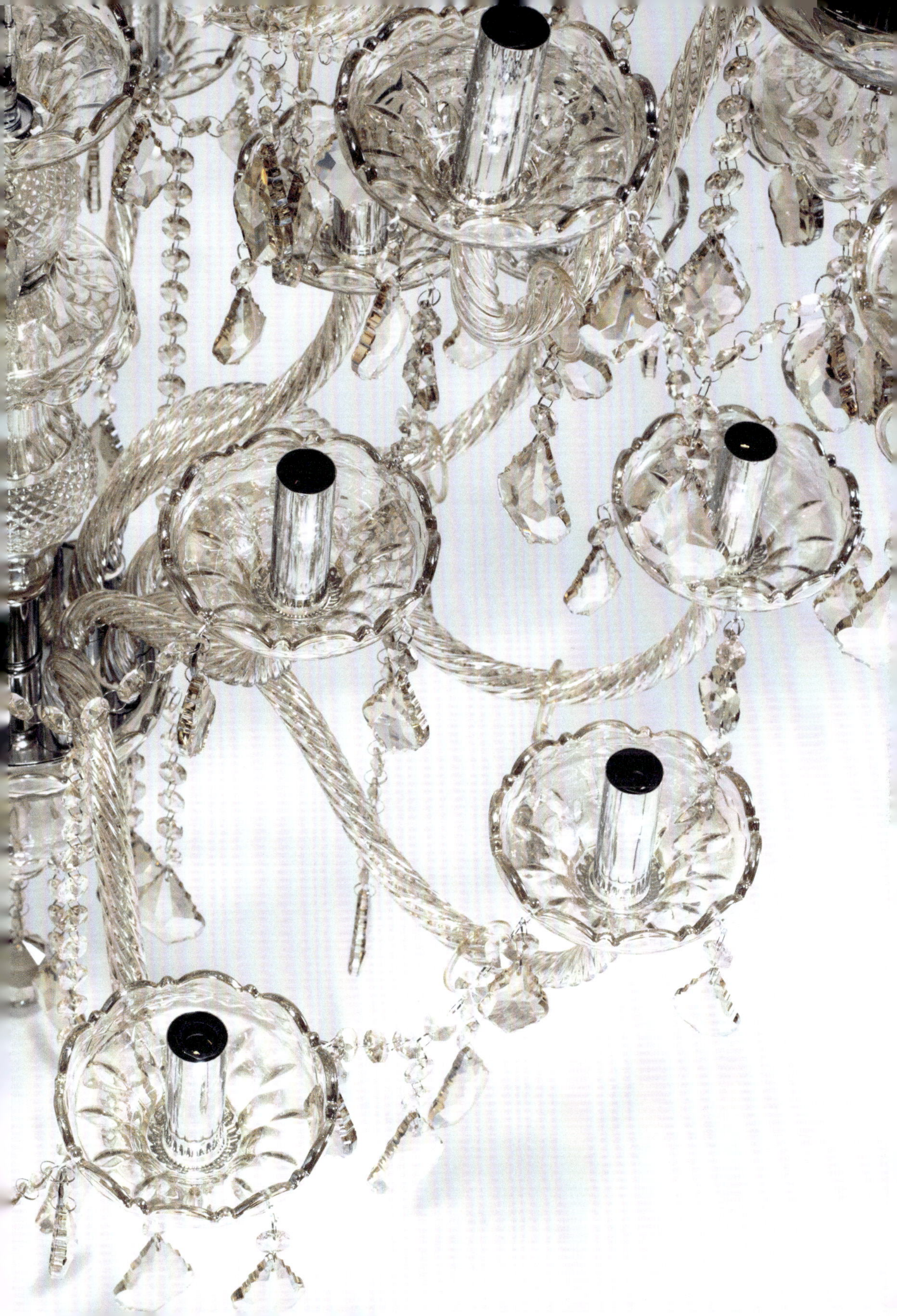

Supreme III, 2023
Hamilton Stands KB400 Classic American Folding Sheet Music Stand (Chrome);
Rhinestone Jewelry Corporation #17012 - Fringe Hoop Earrings - 5"; Crave
Vesper Vibrator Necklace; DOMINATE EMBELLISHED RHINESTONE CHAIN
MAXI DRESS; her hair
54 ¾ × 20 ½ × 17 ¼ inches | 139.1 × 52.1 × 43.8 cm

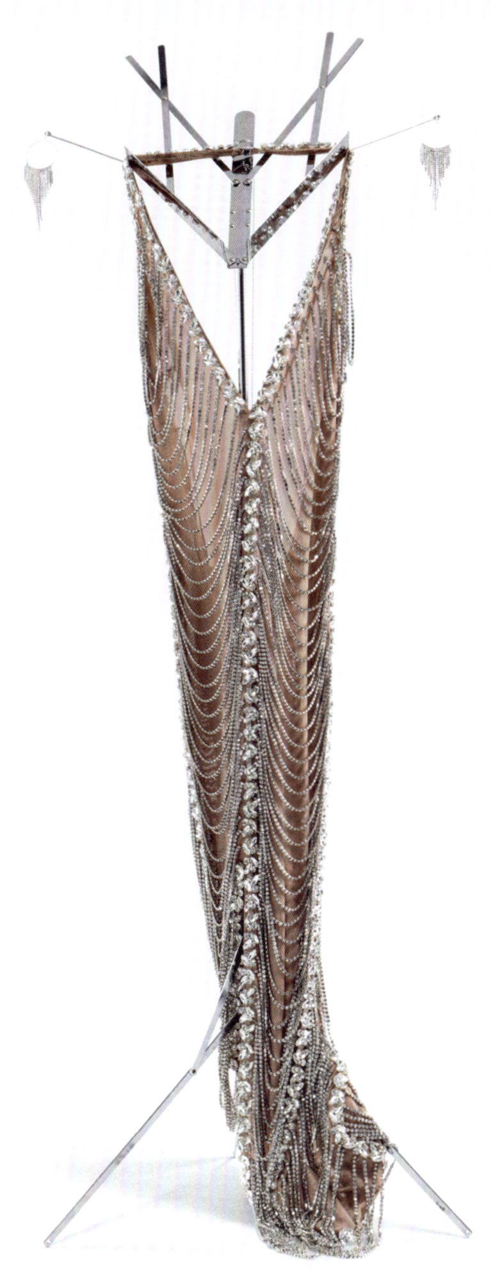

Supreme II, 2023
Hamilton Stands KB400 Classic American Folding Sheet Music Stand (Chrome); boohoo Premium Chainmail Midi Dress GZZ22890-163-34; Heavy Duty Toy Metal Handcuffs with Keys - 6 PACK Stainless Steel Bulk Fake Hand Cuffs Accessories Supplies for Kids Police Pretend Role Play, Adult Party Favors; WXJ13 Swivel Clasps Lanyard Snap Hook Lobster Claw Clasp and Keychain Rings, 55 Pieces; QIYUN.Z (TM) Baroque Vintage Retro Style Faceted Rhinestone Festoon Chandelier Bib Necklace; CITIZEN Ana-Digi Temp JG2101-78E Black Silver Reproduction Men Watch New in Box; Rhinestone Jewelry Corporation #17012 - Fringe Hoop Earrings - 5"
54 ½ × 23 × 18 ¾ inches | 138.4 × 58.4 × 47.6 cm

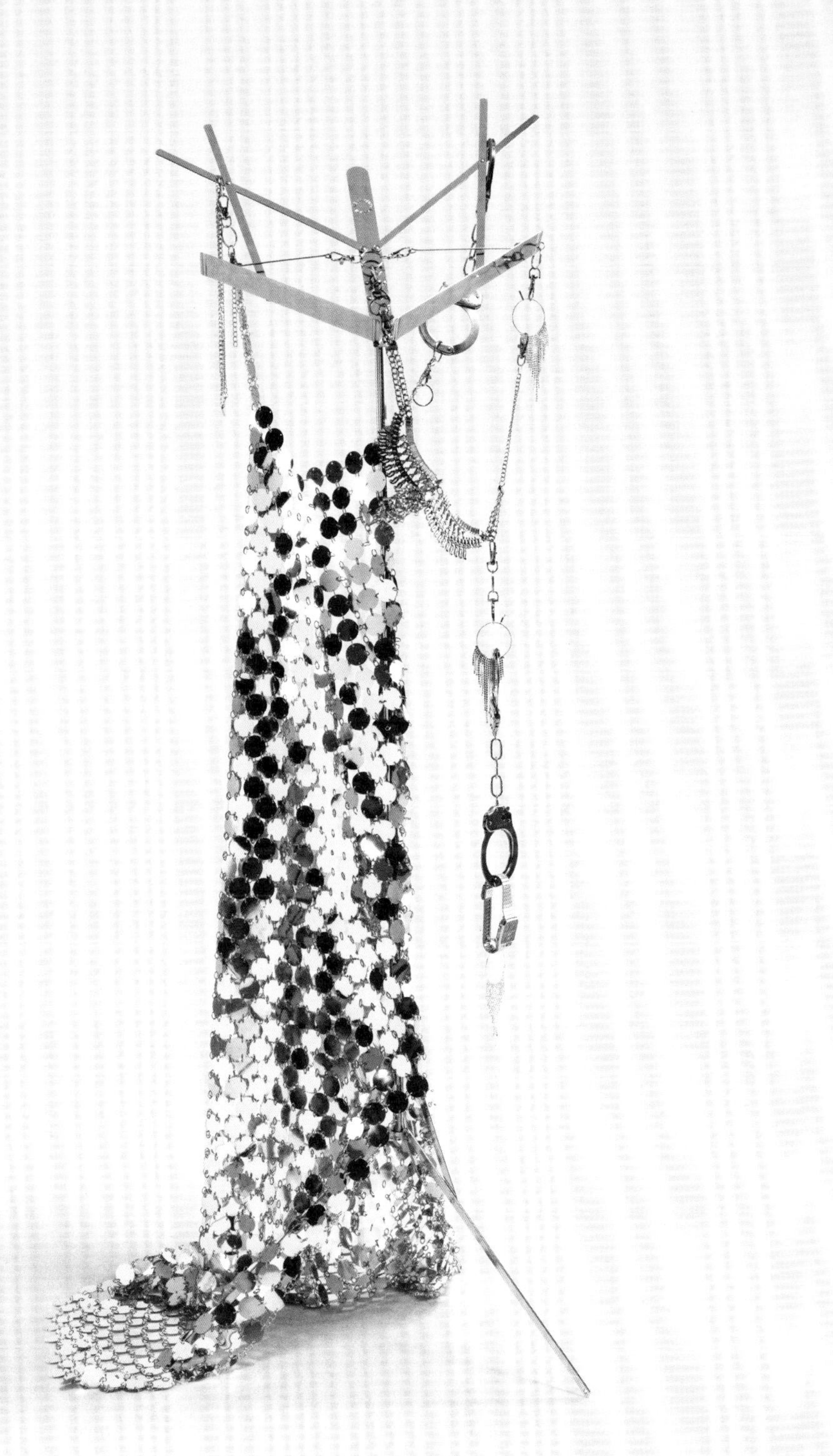

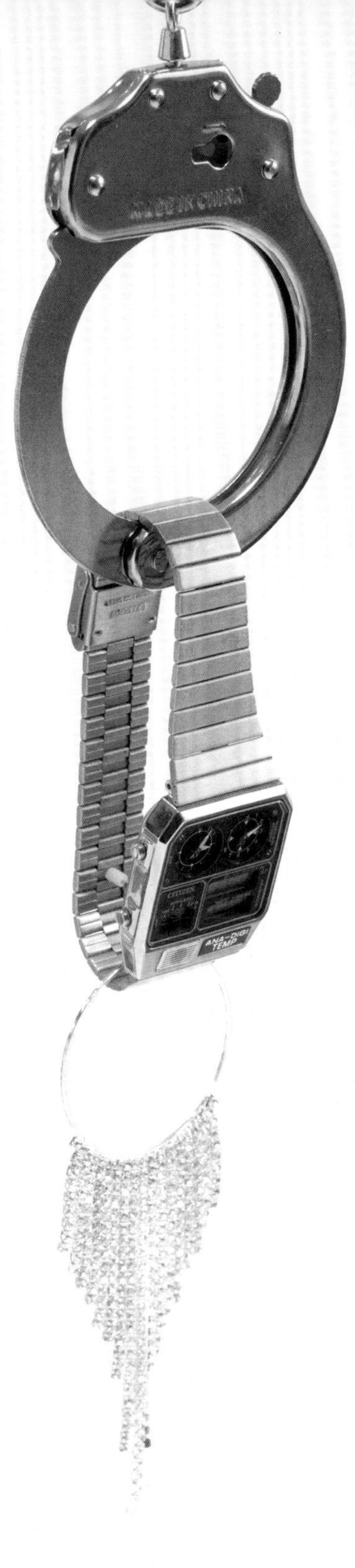

Supreme I, 2023
Hamilton Stands KB400 Classic American Folding Sheet Music Stand (Chrome); Rhinestone Jewelry Corporation #17012 - Fringe Hoop Earrings - 5"; MineSign Rhinestone Choker Necklace Long Tassels Choker Wide Chain Necklace Fashion Jewelry Silver; ZARA TRANSPARENT RESIN TOP; WXJ13 Swivel Clasps Lanyard Snap Hook Lobster Claw Clasp and Keychain Rings, 55 Pieces; GOLDENHAITAI 20pcs 38mm Teardrop Chandelier Crystals, Clear Crystal Chandelier Prisms Pendants Parts Connected Glass Octagon Beads Hanging Garland Decoration
52 ¾ × 23 × 17 ¼ inches | 134 × 58.4 × 43.8 cm

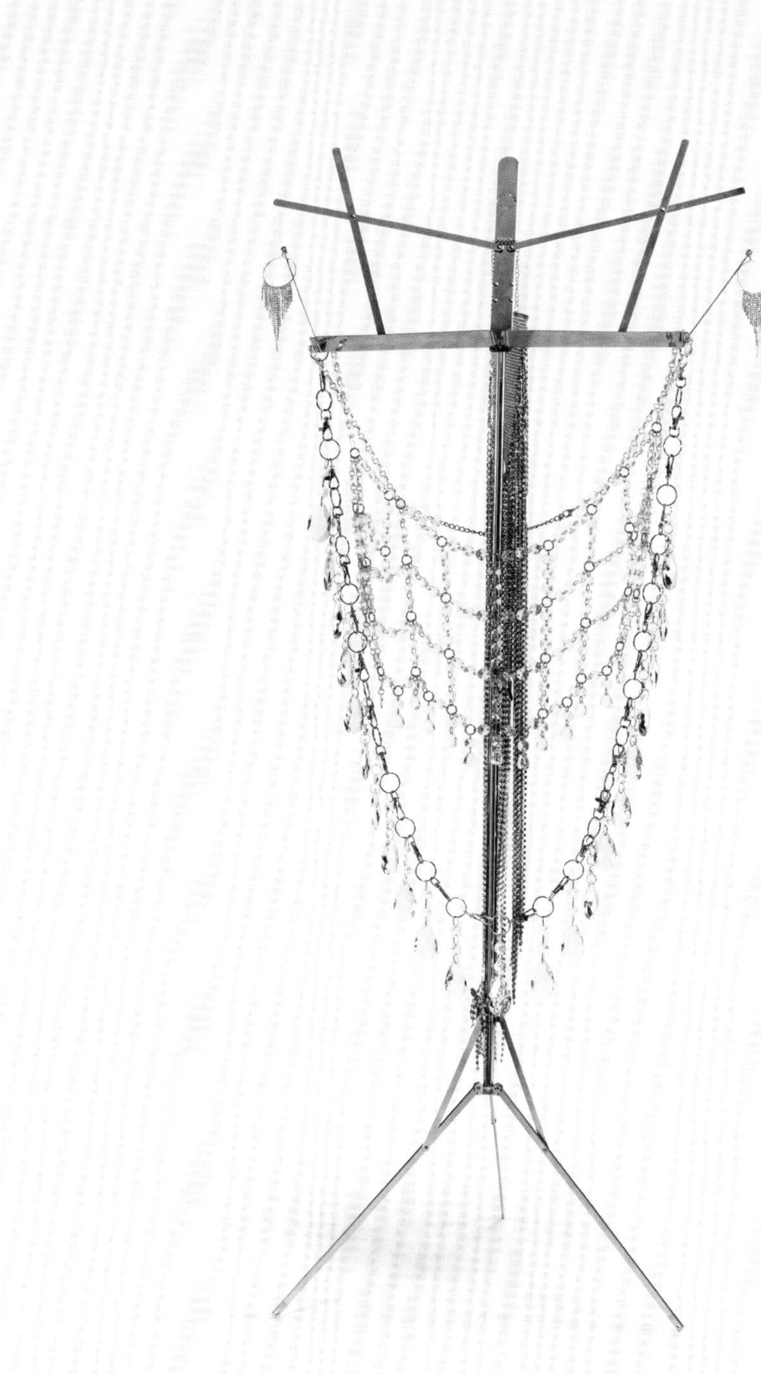

Hunter / Schaeffer, 2023
ASOS DESIGN all over feather sequin embellished long sleeved mini dress in white; Hamilton
Stands KB400 Classic American Folding Sheet Music Stand (Chrome); Premium Diamante
Drop Choker; Denix 6040 1851 Navy Revolver Replica; WXJ13 Swivel Clasps Lanyard
Snap Hook Lobster Claw Clasp and Keychain Rings, 55 Pieces; Heavy Duty Toy Metal Handcuffs
with Keys - 6 PACK Stainless Steel Bulk Fake Hand Cuffs Accessories Supplies for
Kids Police Pretend Role Play, Adult Party Favors
50 ½ × 19 ¼ × 20 ¼ inches | 128.3 × 48.9 × 51.4 cm

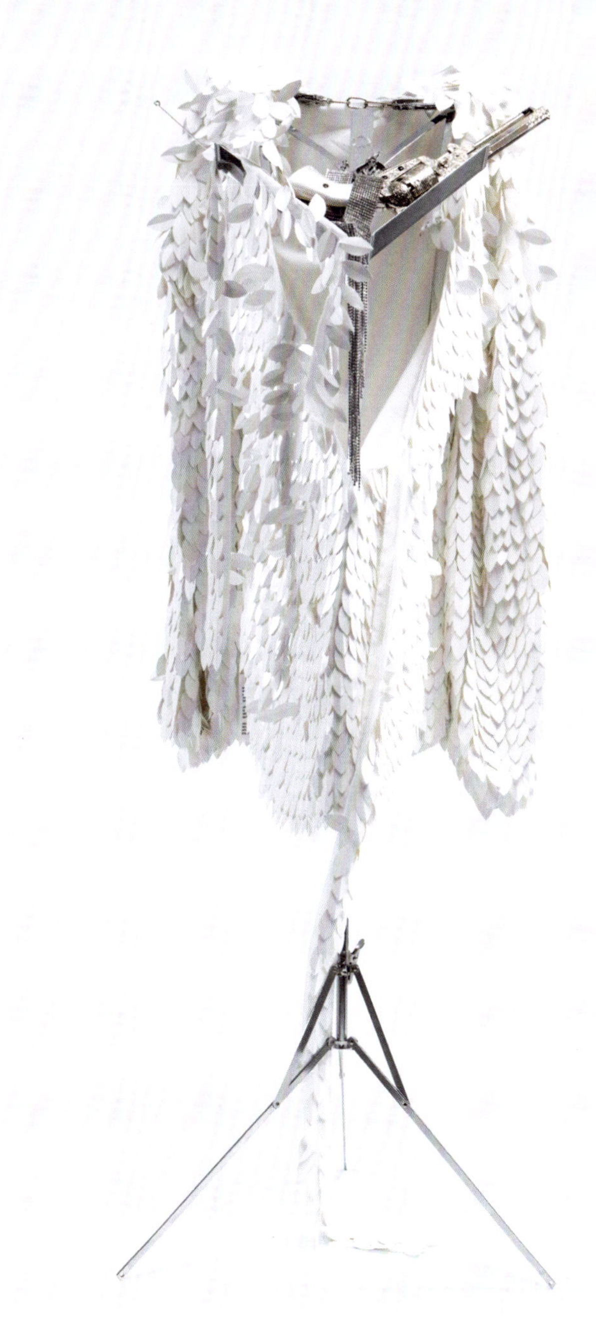

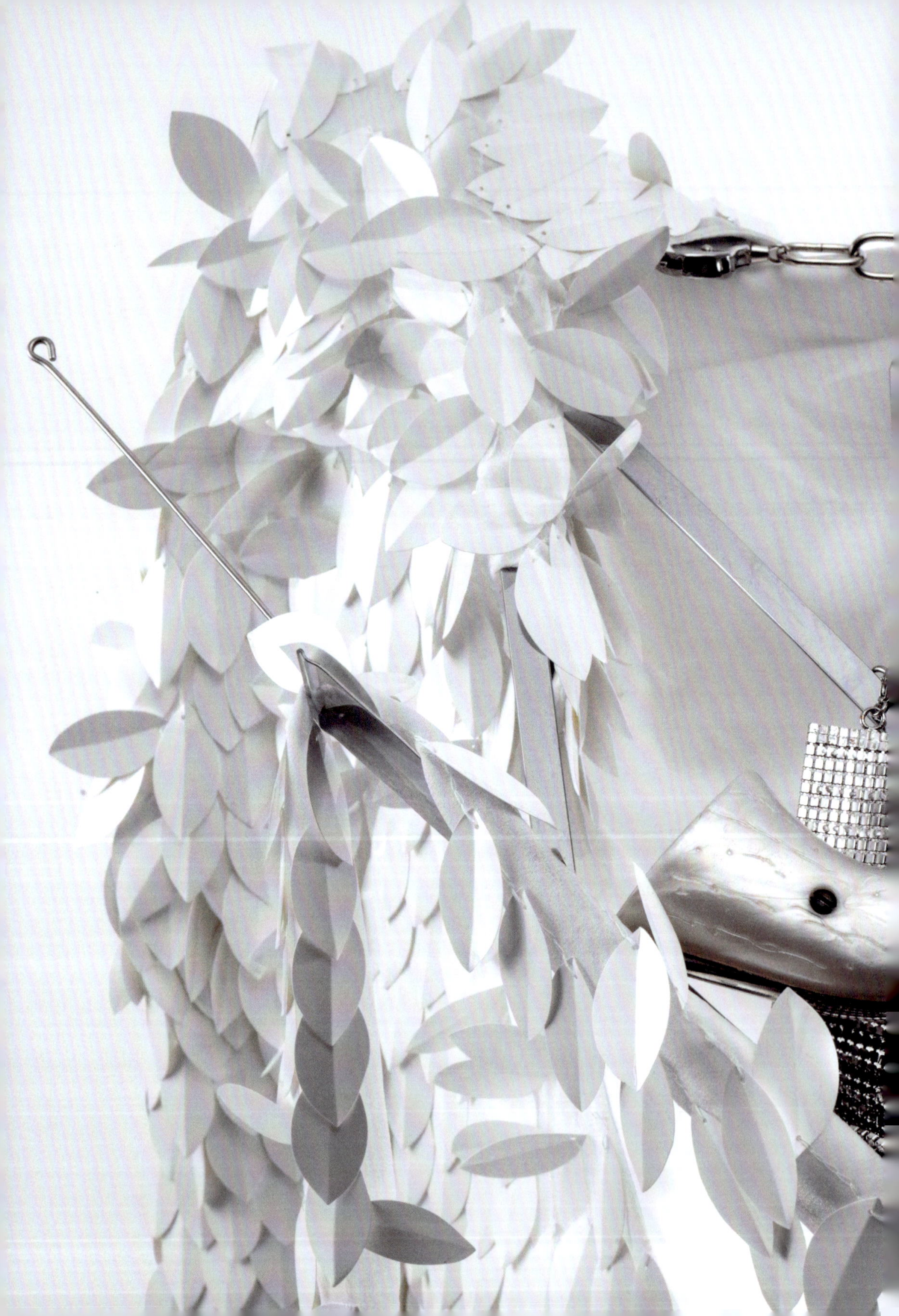

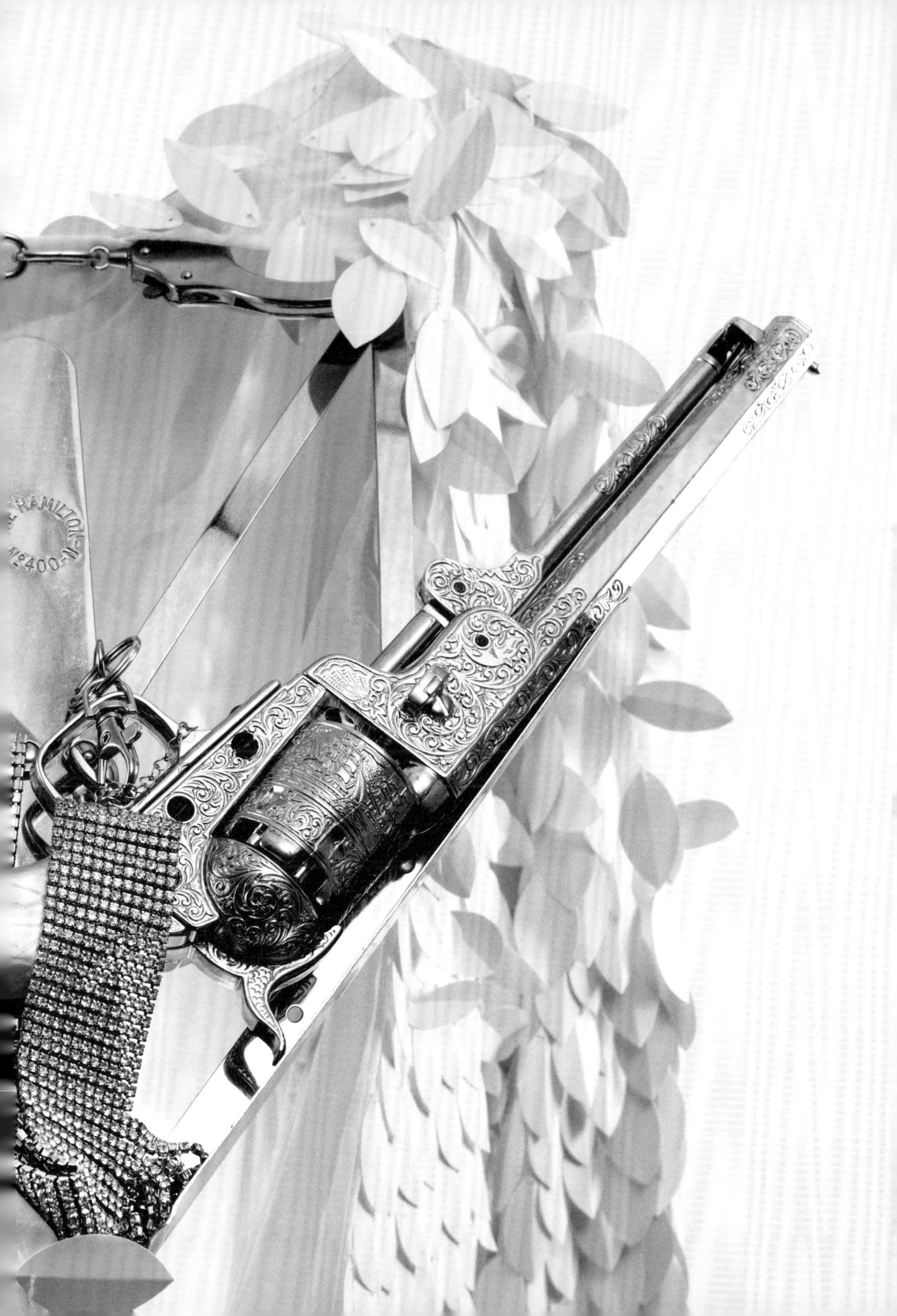

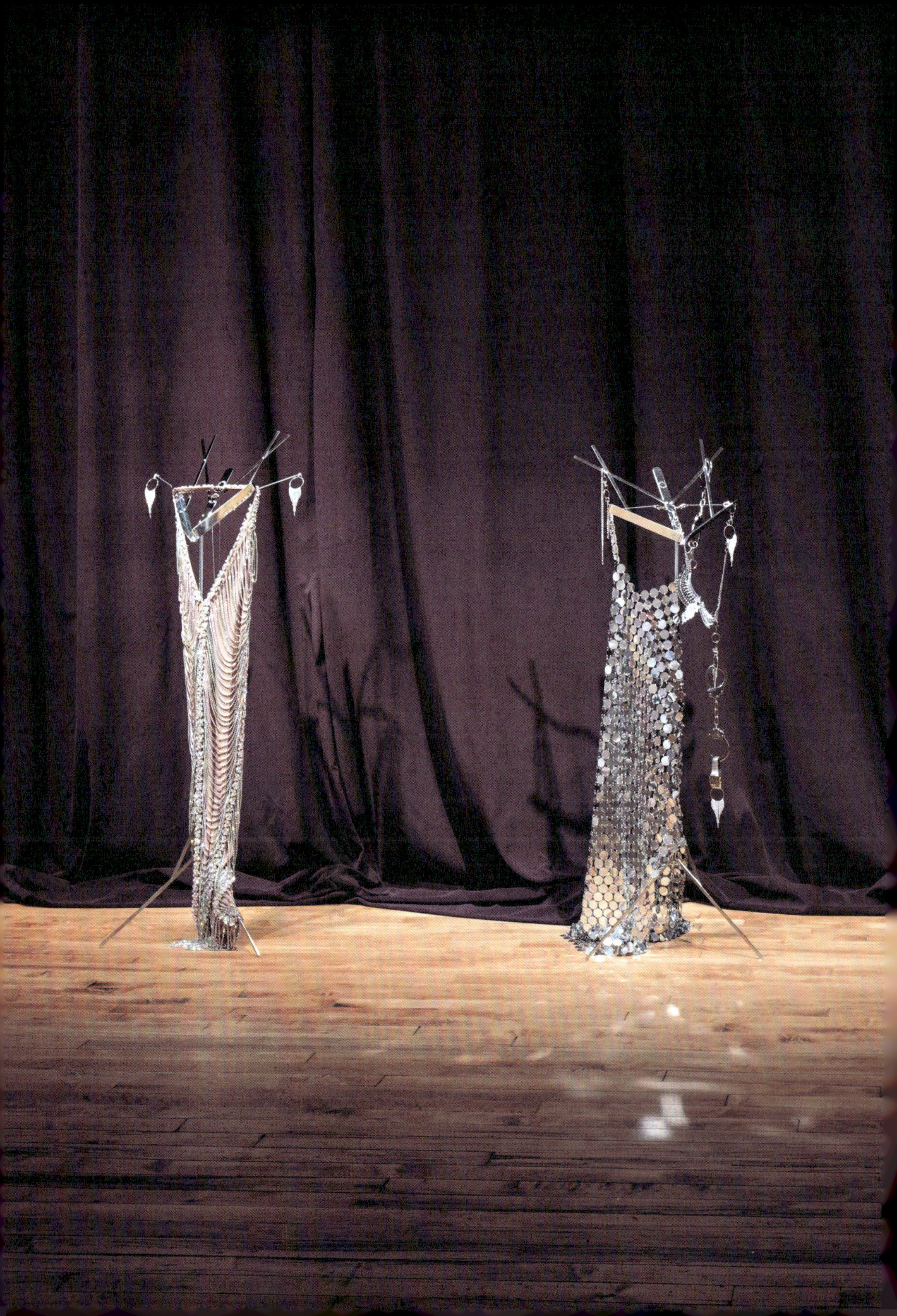

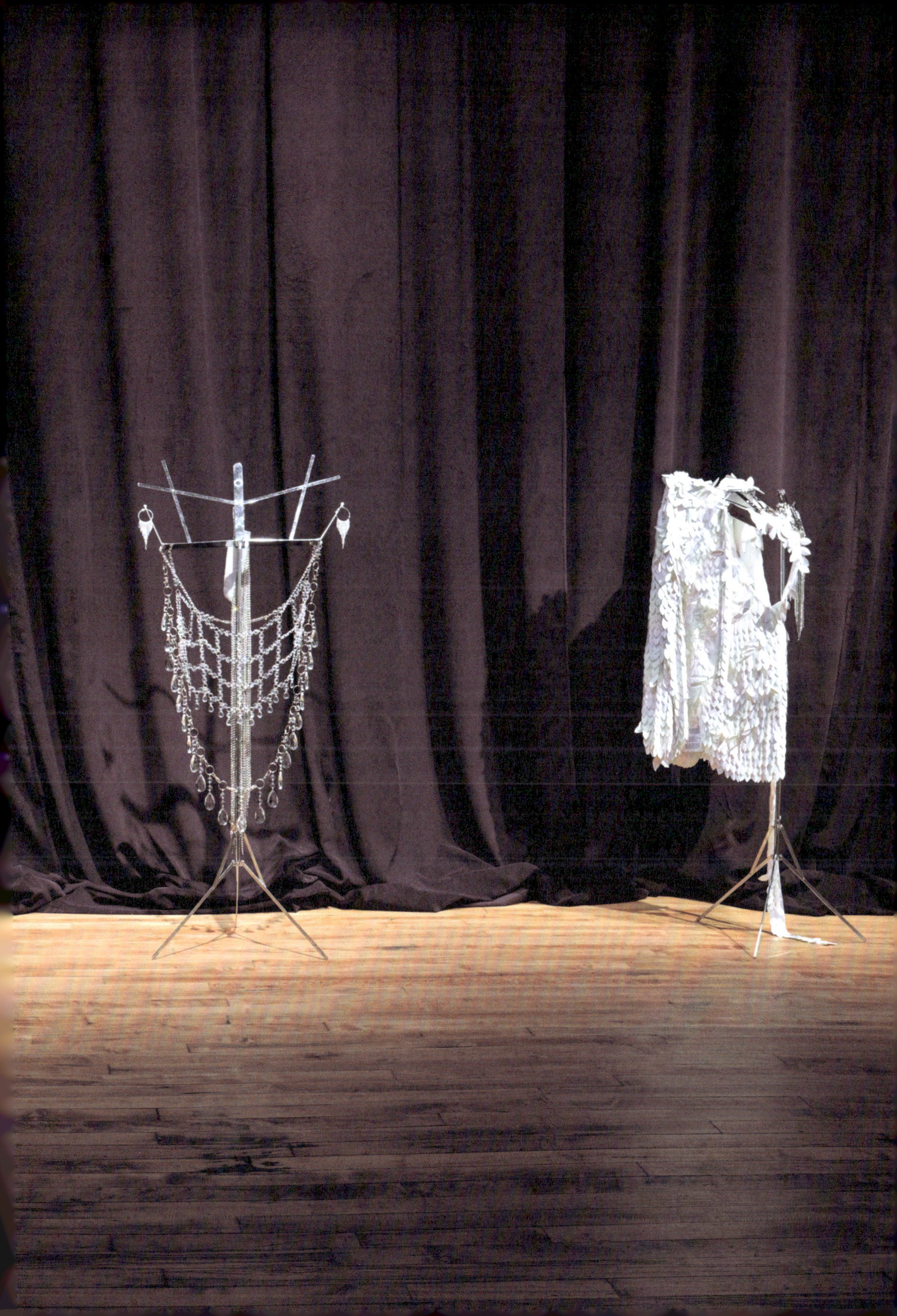

Creature Comfort, 2023
Prevue Pet Products Large Stainless Steel Play Top Bird Cage, Rust Resistant
Metal Cage for Birds with Rooftop Ladder and Playtop; Denix Desert Eagle
Non-Firing Prop Replica Pistol in Nickel Finish
63 × 31 ½ × 24 inches | 160 × 80 × 61 cm

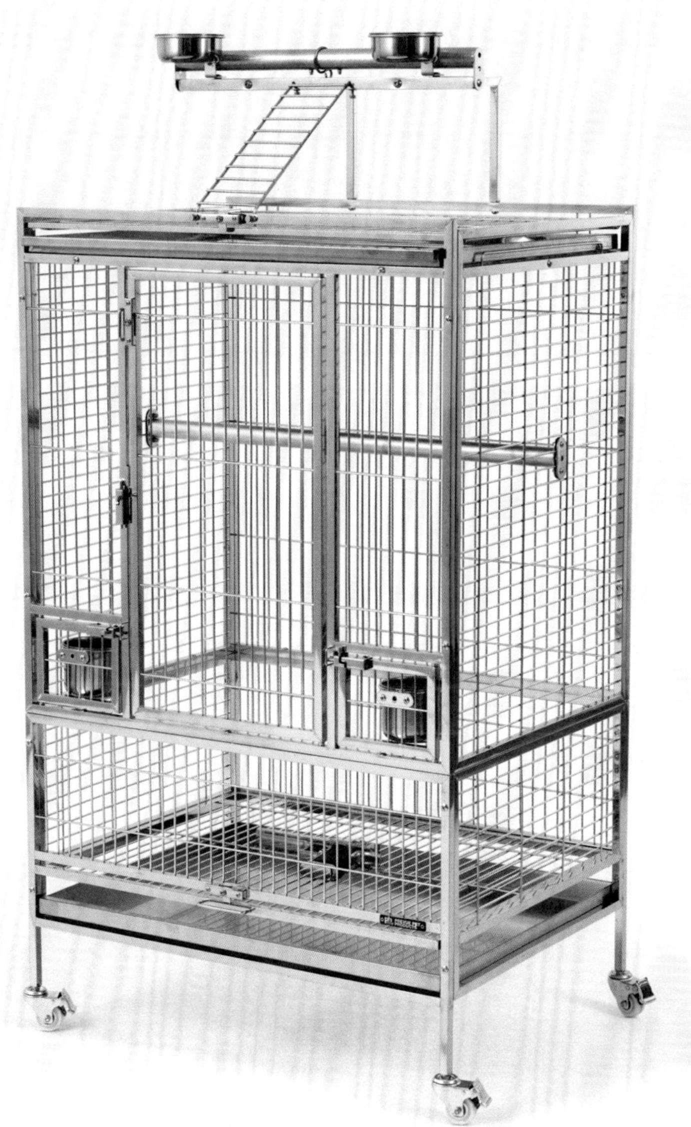

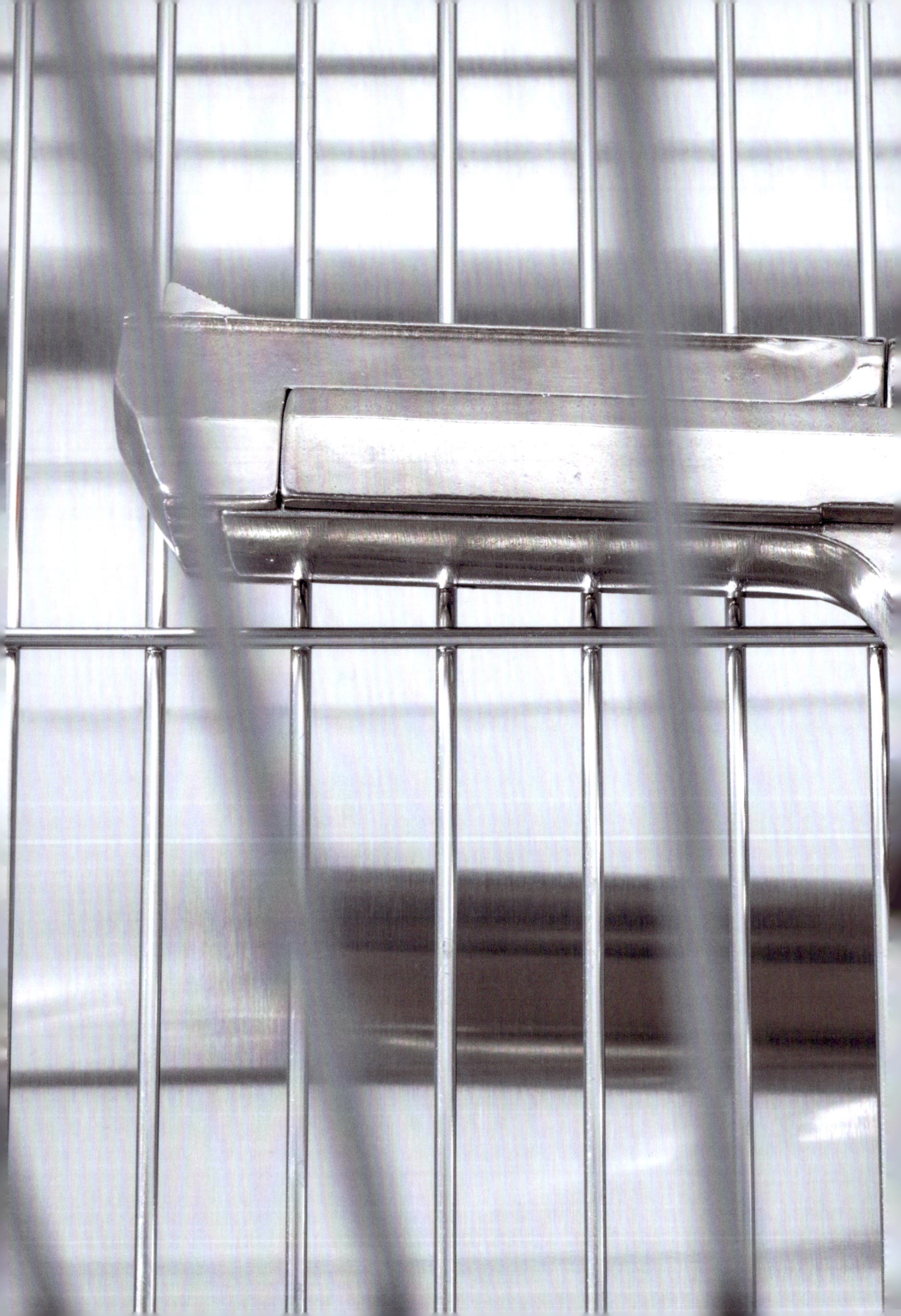

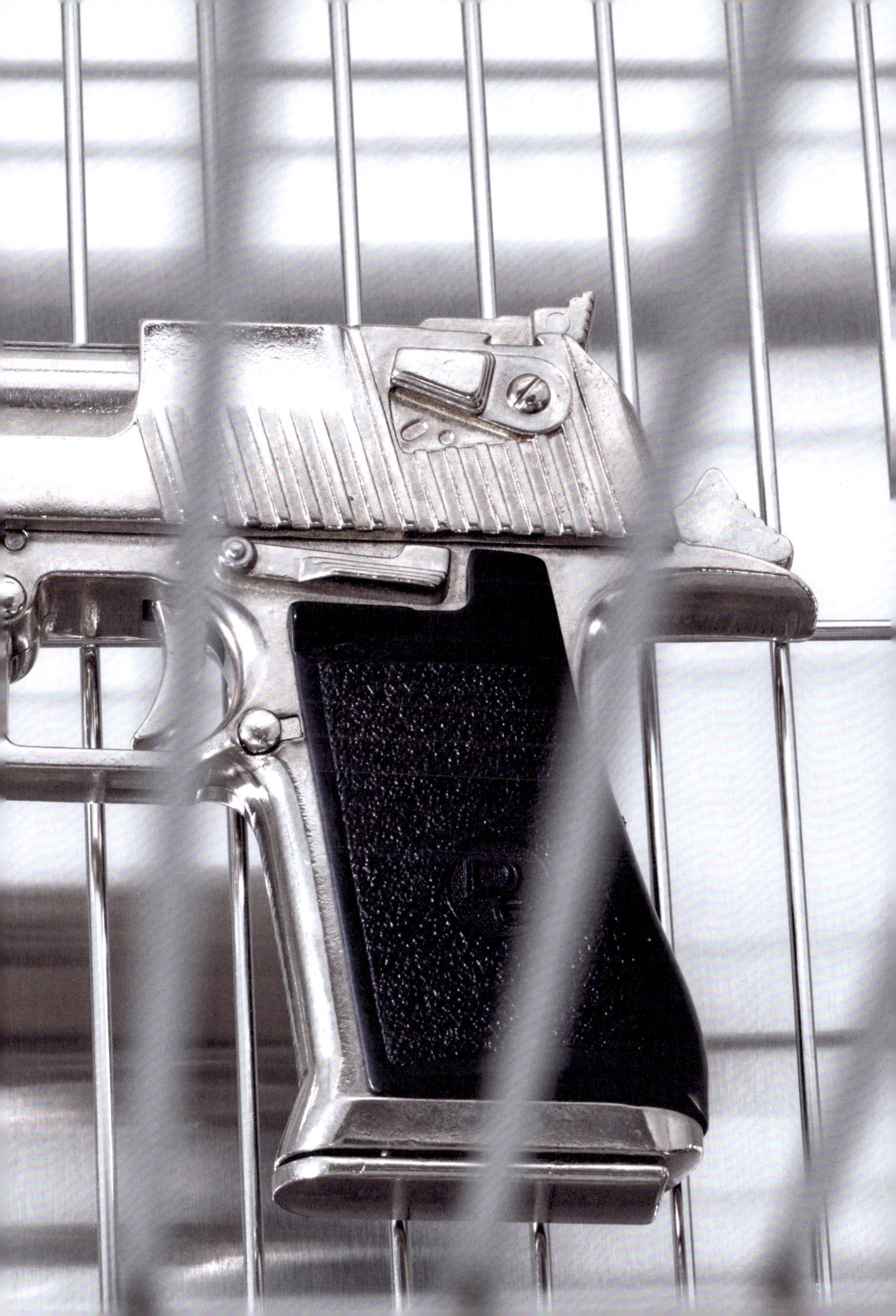

Before Christmas, 2023
Staveley 70" Silver Arched/Arc Floor Lamp; Victorinox swiss army knives
silvertech; Pearl Crystal Beat Bass Drum - 24 x 14 inch - Ultra Clear; hardware
76 ¼ × 66 × 19 ½ inches | 193.7 × 167.6 × 49.5 cm

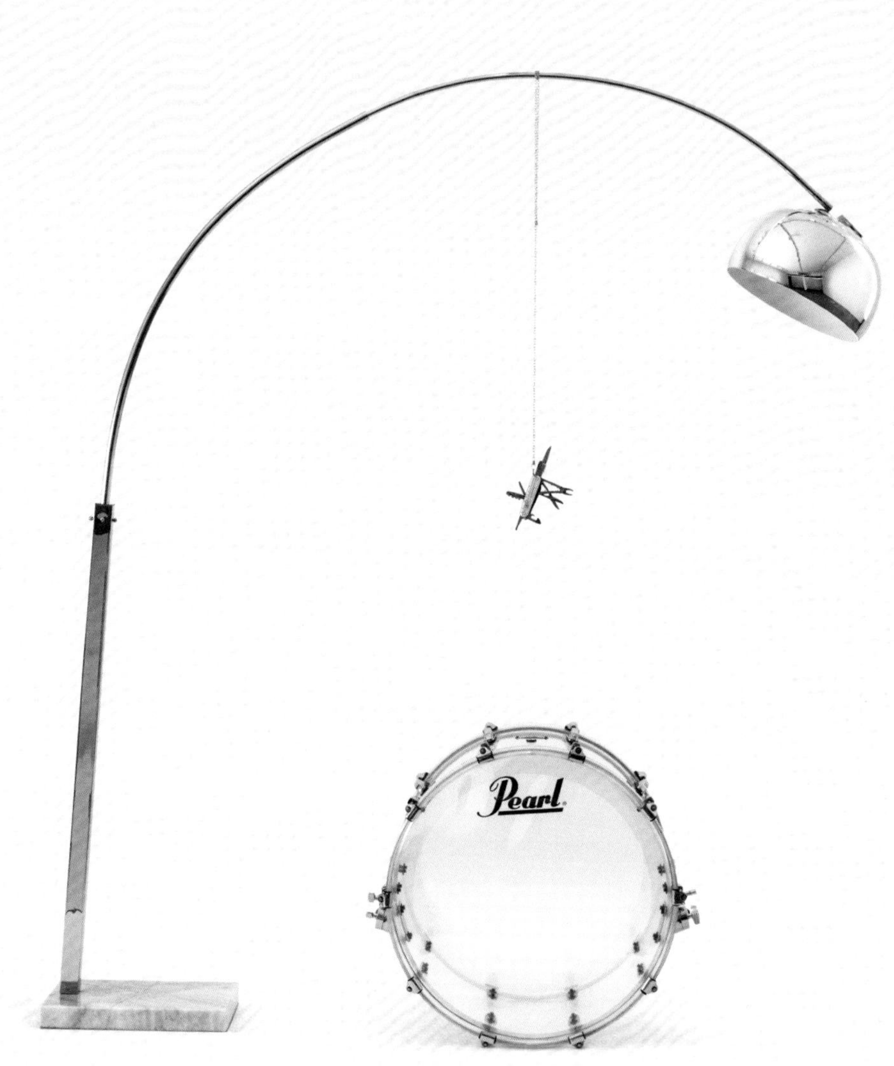
Pearl

Adam's Song (Norm), 2023
Aluminum Hard Case Briefcase Box Lockable Flight Case Carrying Tools
Container for Test Instruments Cameras Tools Mechanical Garage Silver; The
Spirit-Filled Life Bible, New King James Version; Petite Club Chair - Espresso
Brown Leather Inspired By: Le Corbusier LC2 Chair); Andrew Norman Wilson
23 × 30 × 27 ¾ inches | 58.4 × 76.2 × 70.5 cm

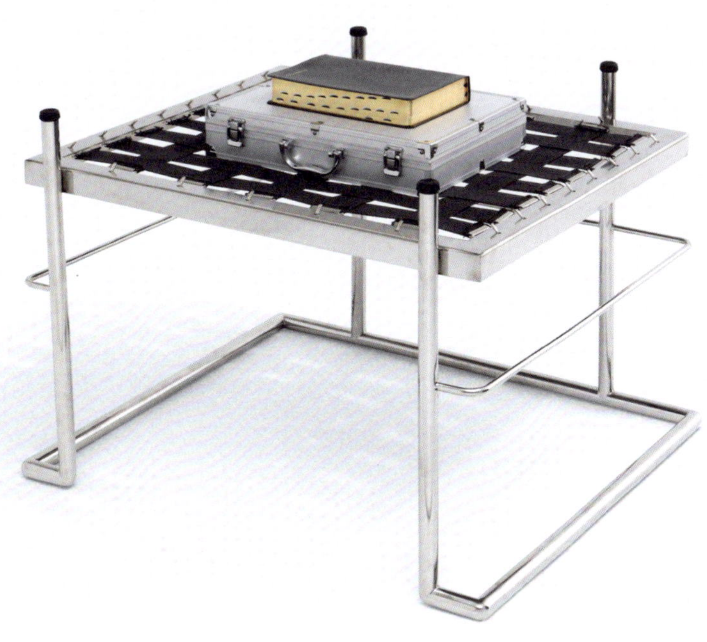

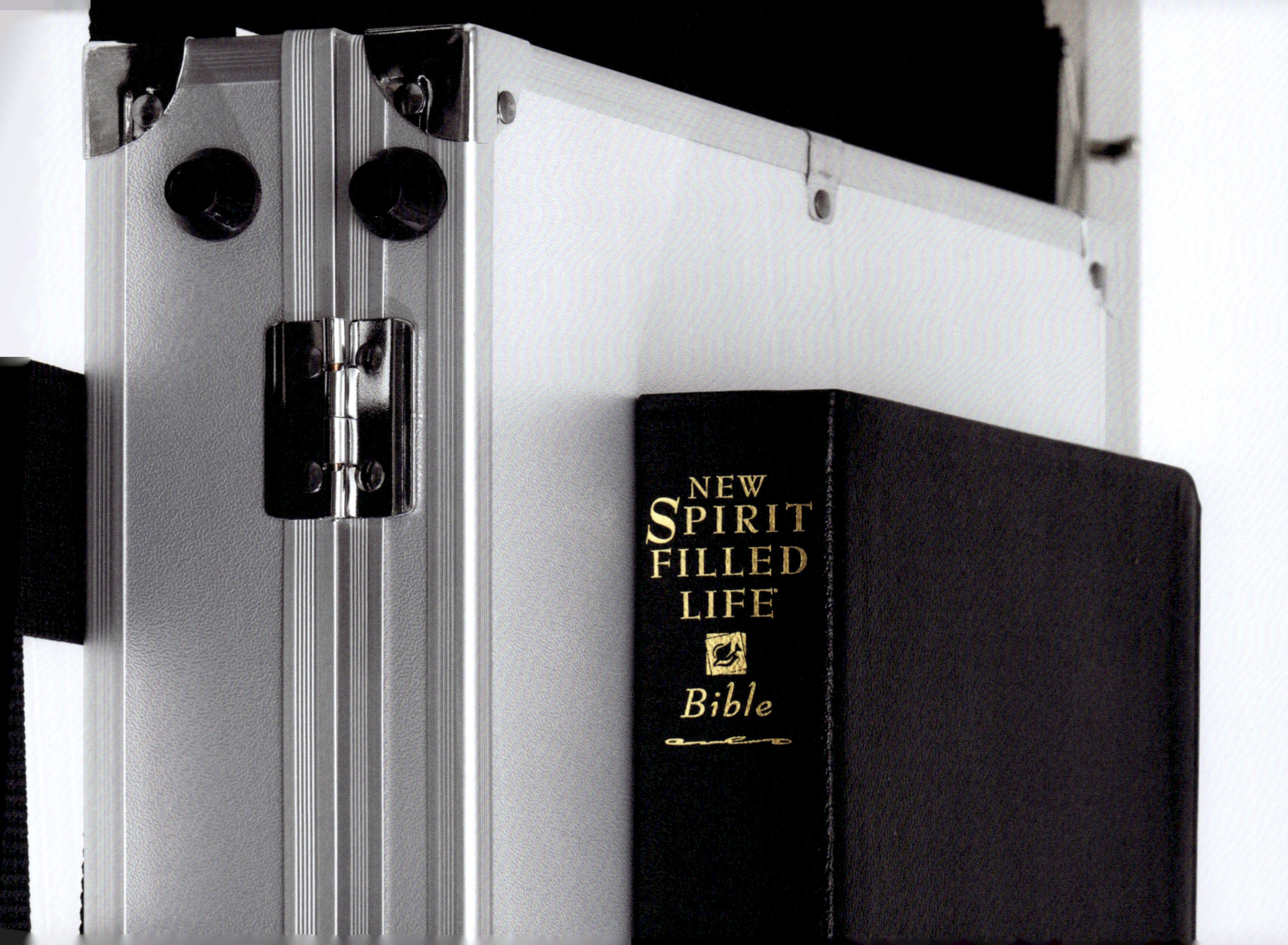

NEW
SPIRIT
FILLED
LIFE
Bible

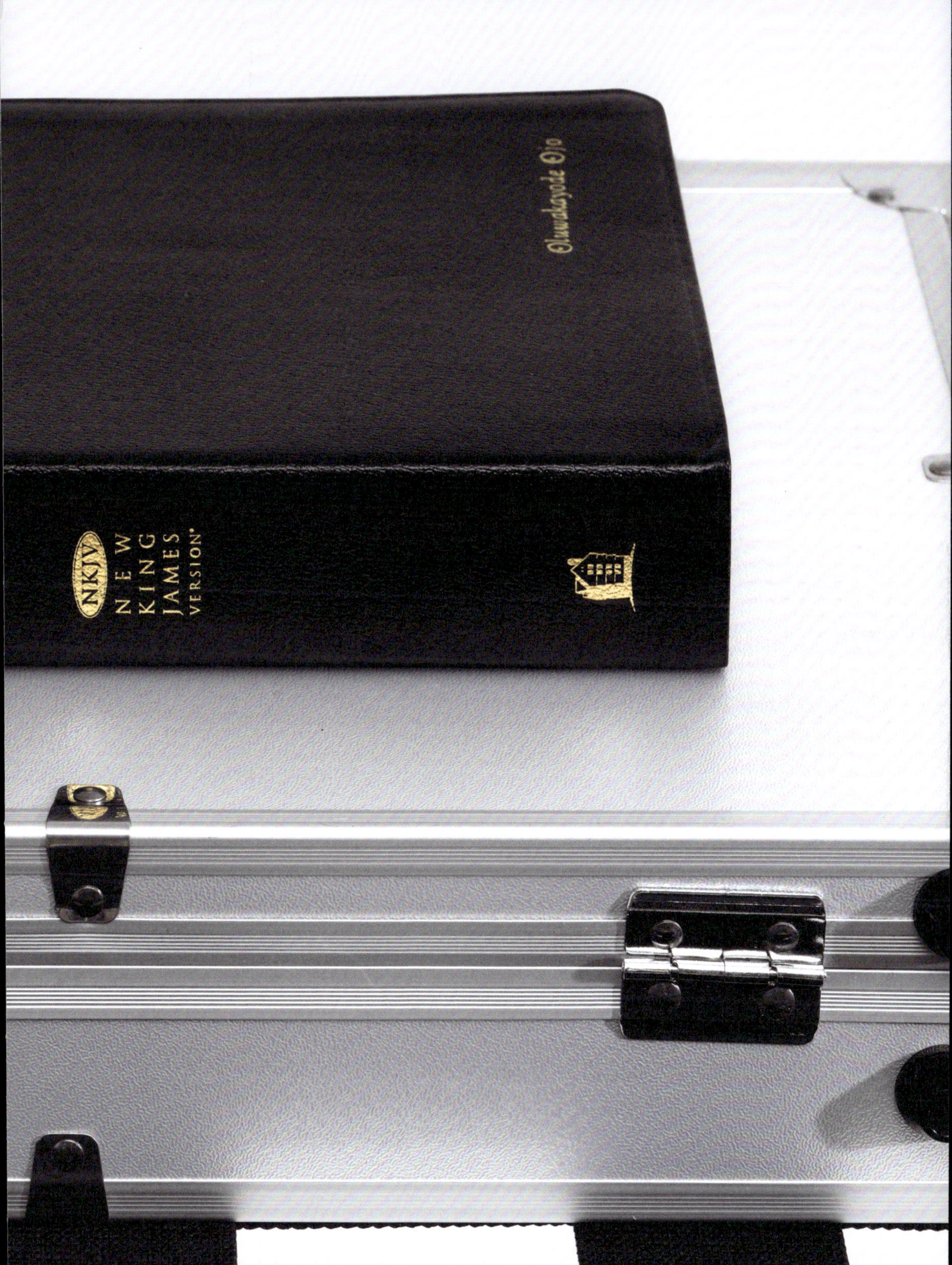

Oluwakayode Ojo
NKJV
NEW KING JAMES VERSION

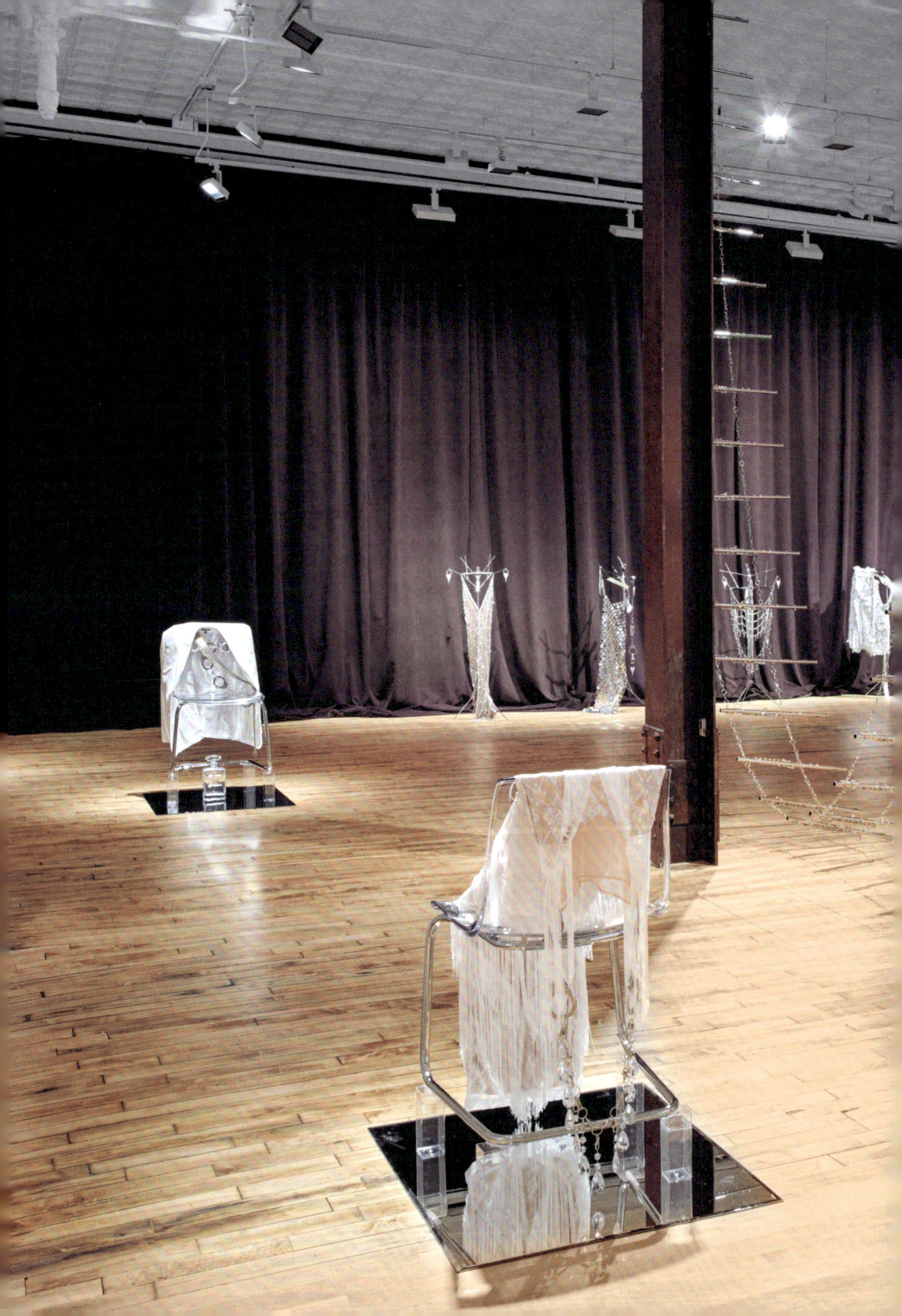

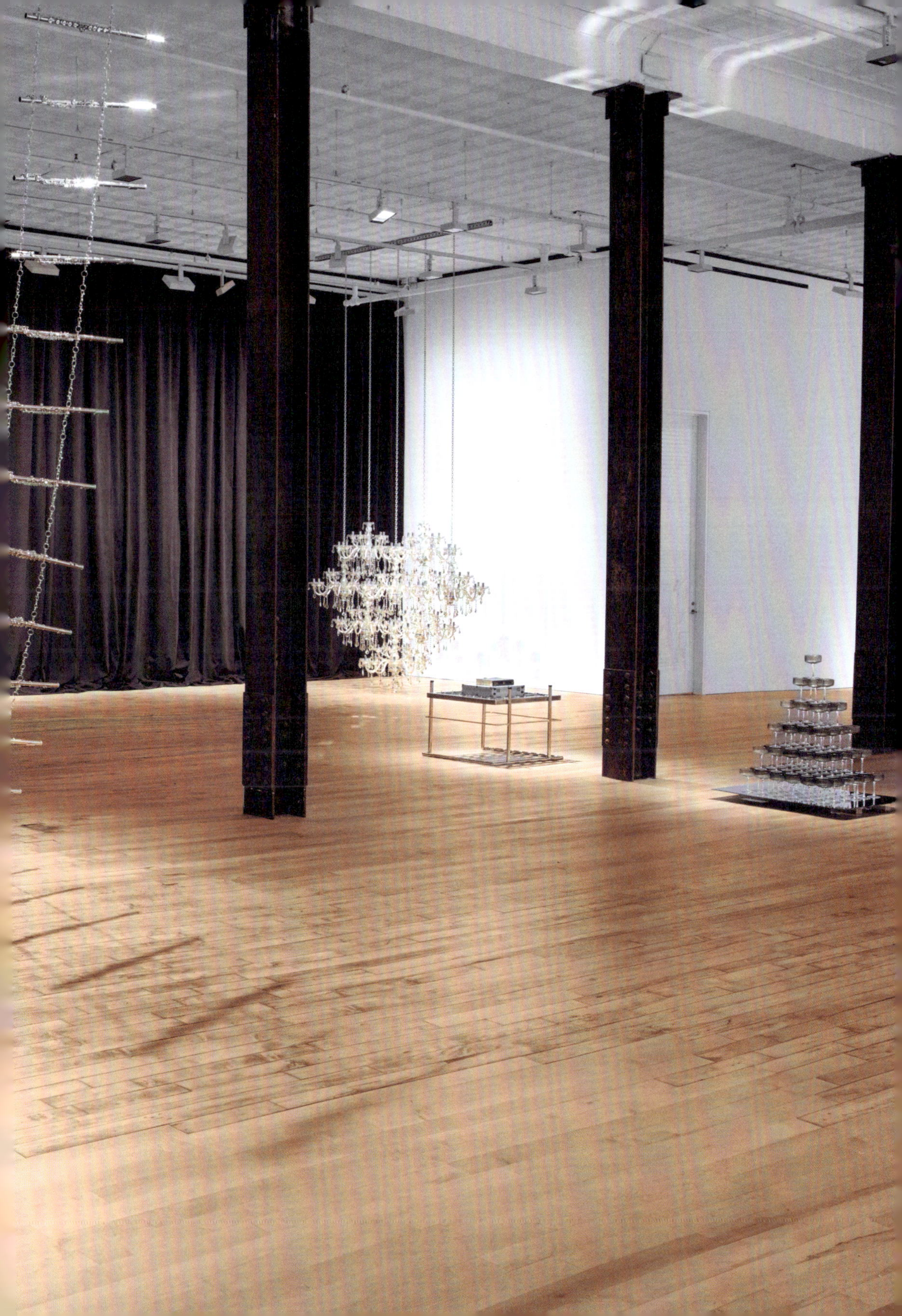

Obasanjo (Taylor's Version) (Tribeca), 2023
SHEIN Fringe Trim Lace Overlay Dress Only 5 Left; Heavy Duty Toy Metal Handcuffs
with Keys - 6 PACK Stainless Steel Bulk Fake Hand Cuffs Accessories Supplies
for Kids Police Pretend Role Play, Adult Party Favors; WXJ13 Swivel Clasps Lanyard
Snap Hook Lobster Claw Clasp and Keychain Rings, 55 Pieces; GOLDENHAITAI 20pcs
38mm Teardrop Chandelier Crystals, Clear Crystal Chandelier Prisms Pendants Parts
Connected Glass Octagon Beads Hanging Garland Decoration; NWT Express
White (Ivory) Velvet Tuxedo Jacket; M16 .223 bullet belt - Full Silver w/Silver link;
Godinger Reserve Whiskey Decanter for Liquor Scotch Bourbon - 40oz Clear; Tobias
Chairs; Clear Amac Boxes; Glacier Bay Beveled Edge Bath Mirrors
Overall dimensions variable

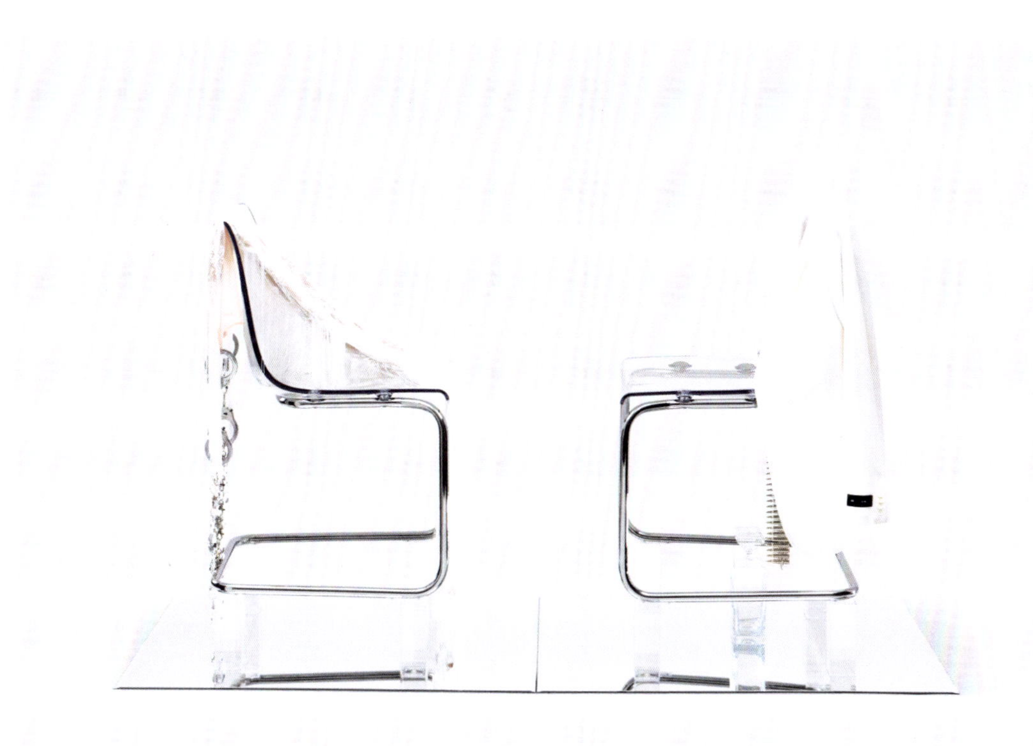

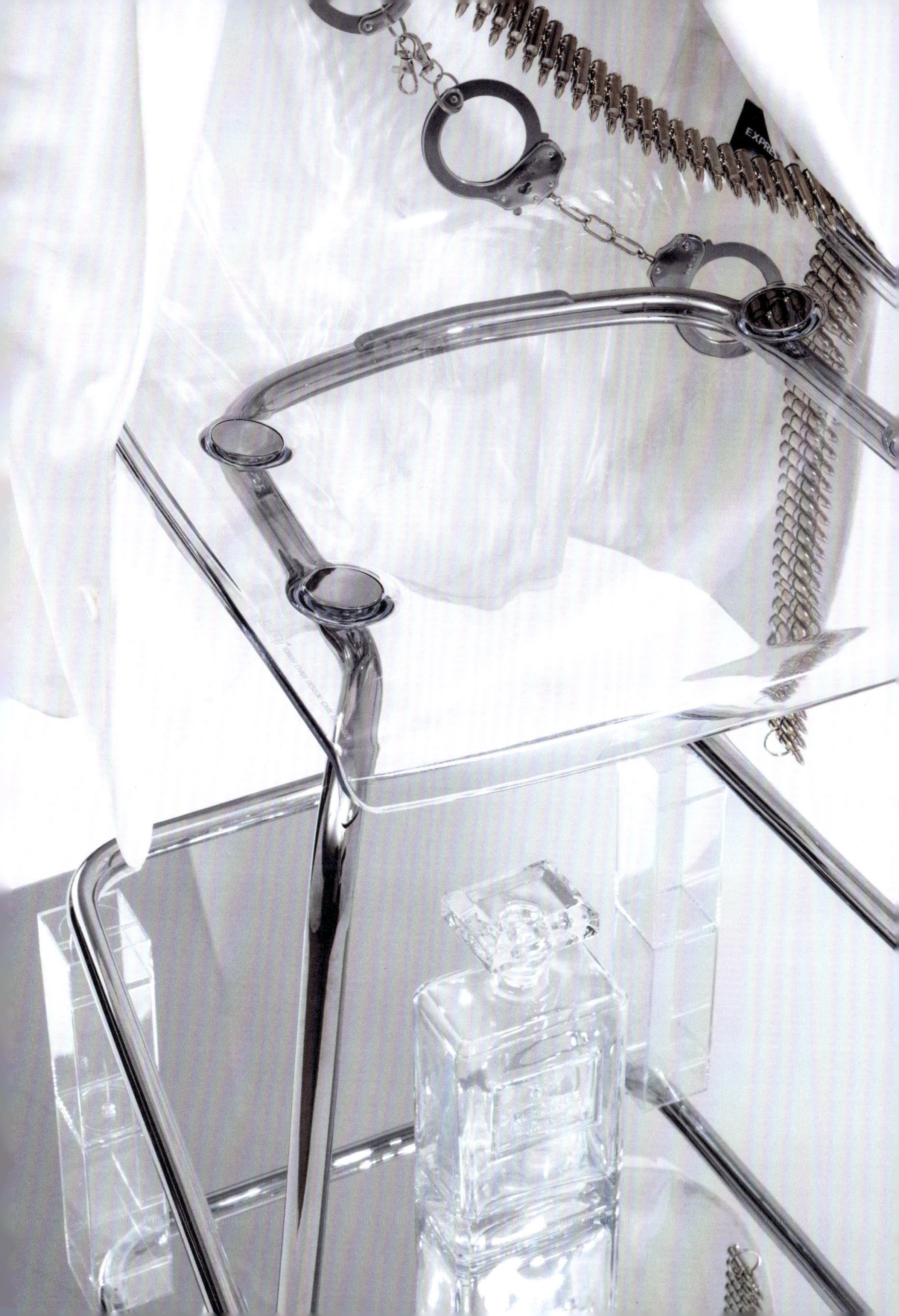

Embouchure ('ɪzoʊ), 2023
Glory Closed Hole C Flute With Case, Tuning Rod and Cloth, Joint
Grease and Gloves Nickel Silver; WXJ13 Swivel Clasps Lanyard Snap
Hook Lobster Claw Clasp and Keychain Rings, 55 Pieces
Overall dimensions variable

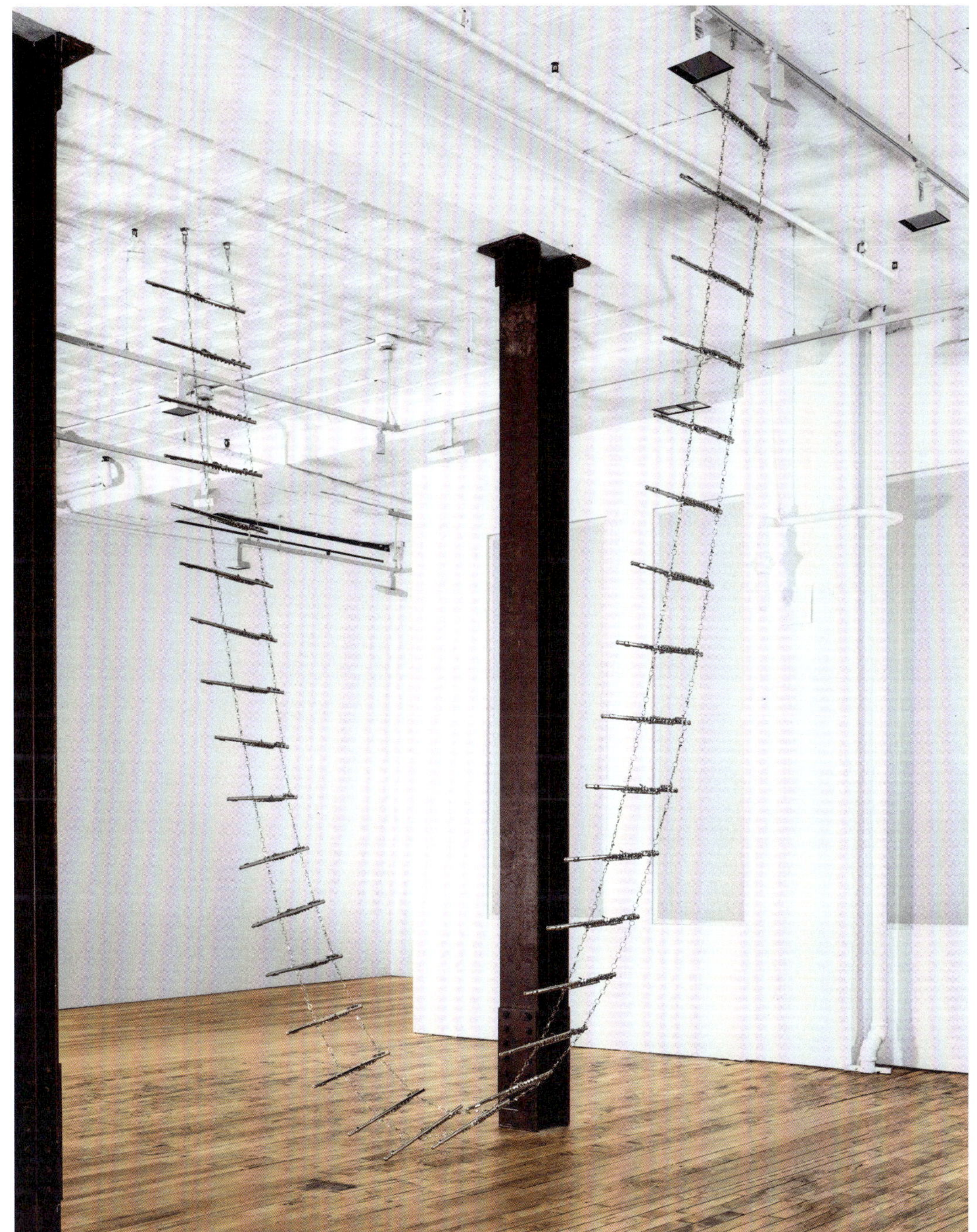

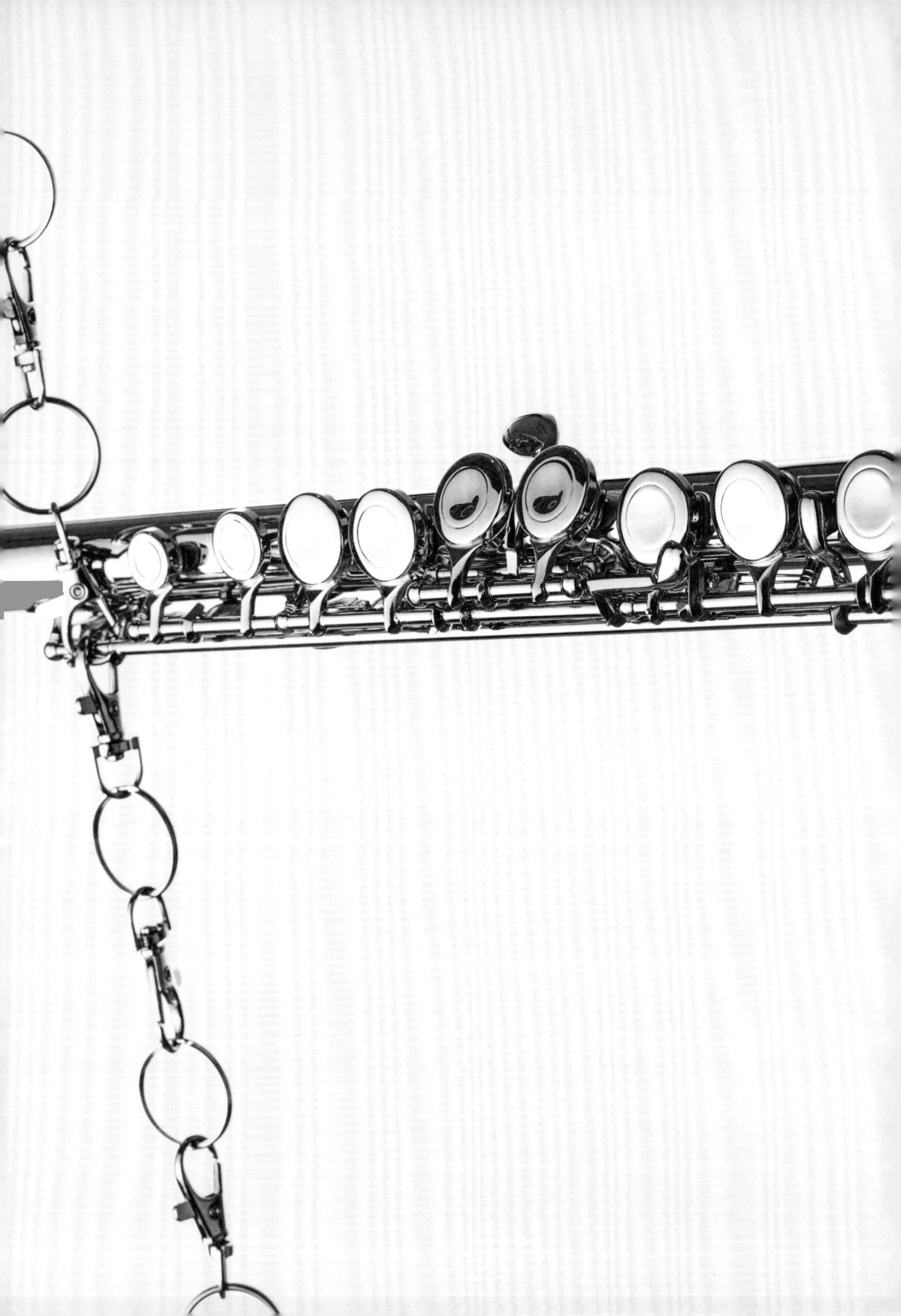

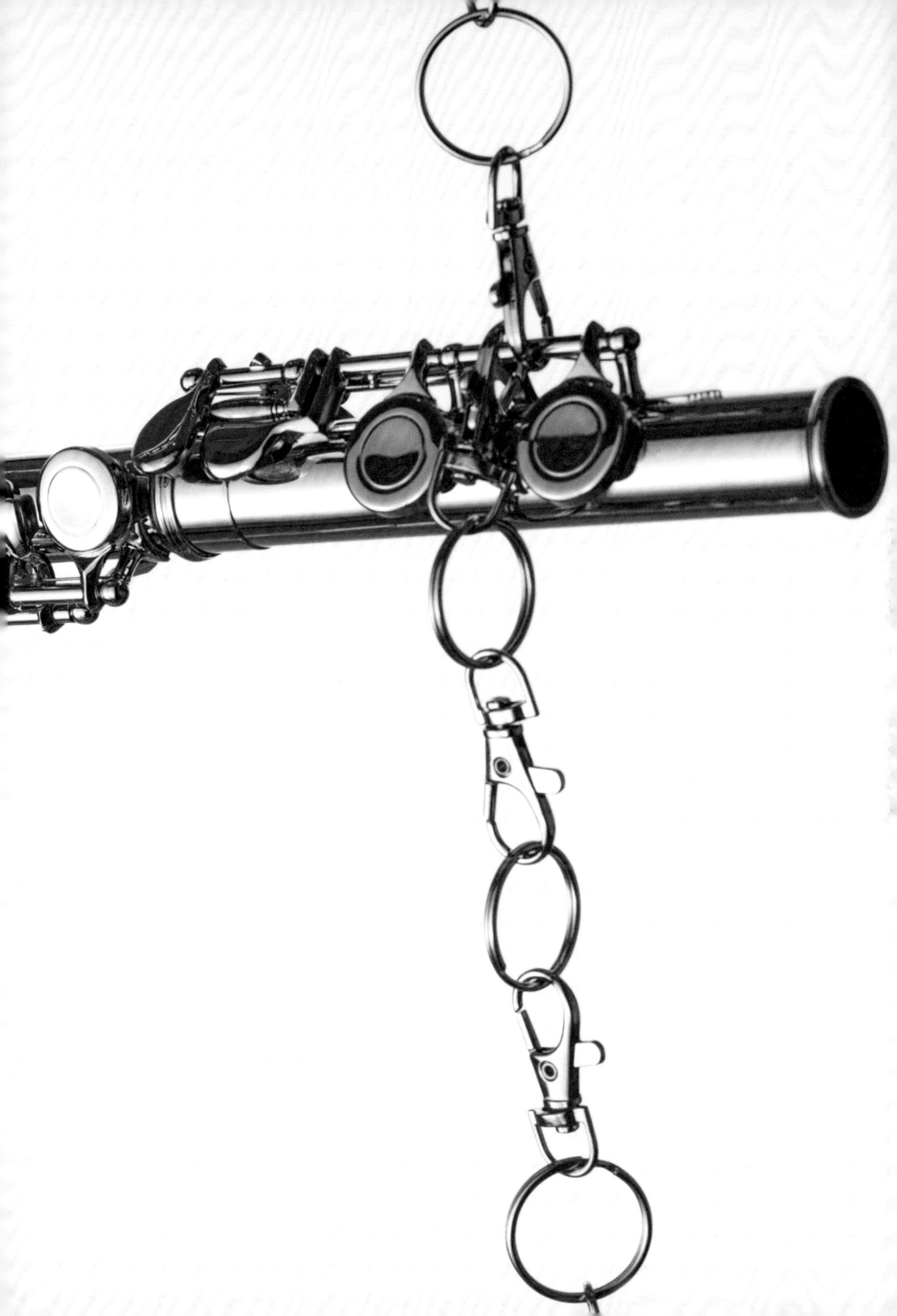

Edit sober, 2023
Bromine Element - Acrylic Element Cube ProtoshopLLC; Godinger Reserve
Whiskey Decanter for Liquor Scotch Bourbon - 40oz Clear; Hermes 3000
Seafoam Green Working Typewriter & Case w/Manual - Free Shipping to Lower
48!; Acrylic transparent B flat 17 key student clarinet silver plated keys; Glacier
Bay Frameless Rectangular Beveled Edge Bathroom Vanity Mirror in Silver
$11 \times 48 \times 13\,\frac{3}{4}$ inches | $27.9 \times 121.9 \times 34.9$ cm

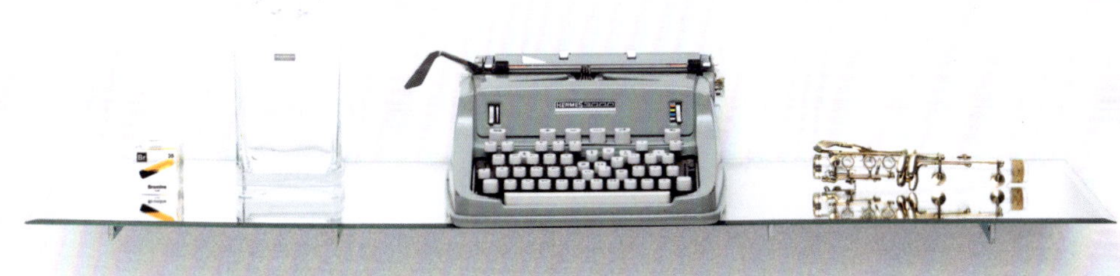

The Brick, 2023
SWAN Harmonica in C Key 10 Holes 40 Tone Mouth Organ Stainless Steel
Chromatics Harmonica SW1040; Argus C3 with a 50mm f/3.5 Range Finder
35mm Film Camera; Godinger Airplane Cocktail Shaker – New; FAREVER
Melting Clock, Salvador Dali Watch Melted Clock for Decorative Home
Office Shelf Desk Table Funny Creative Gift, Rome; Glacier Bay Frameless
Rectangular Beveled Edge Bathroom Vanity Mirror in Silver
16 ½ × 48 × 14 inches | 41.9 × 121.9 × 35.6 cm

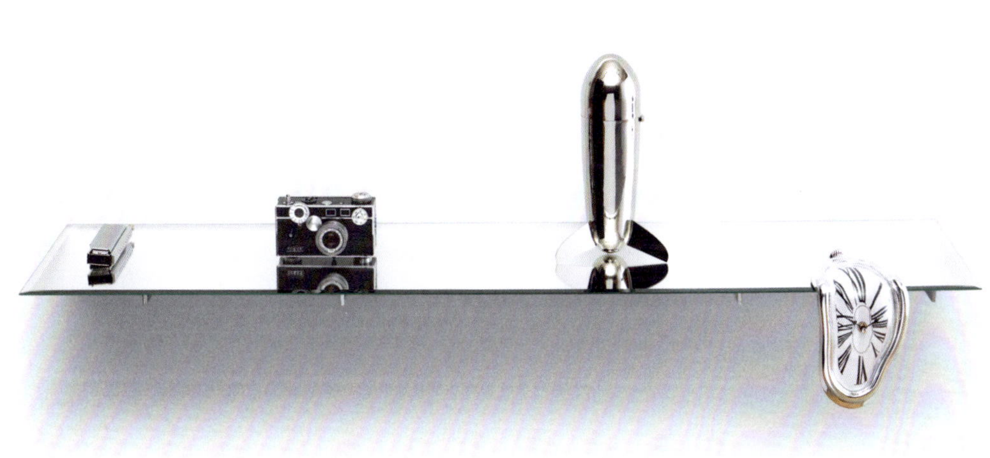

Comfort, 2023
New Orleans 4 -Light Clear Unique/Statement Geometric
Chandelier with Crystal Accents
84 × 72 × 16 inches | 213.4 × 182.9 × 40.6 cm

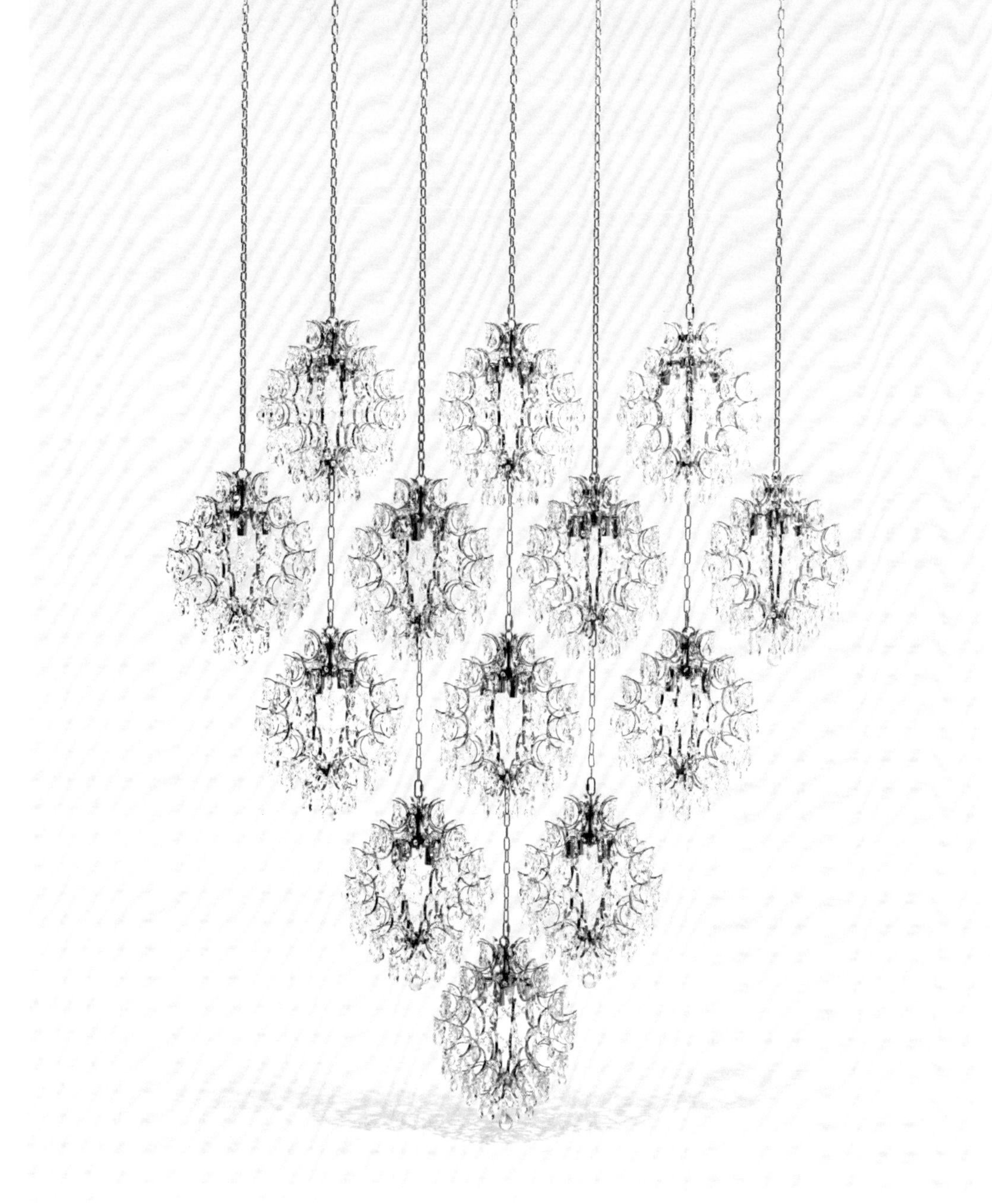

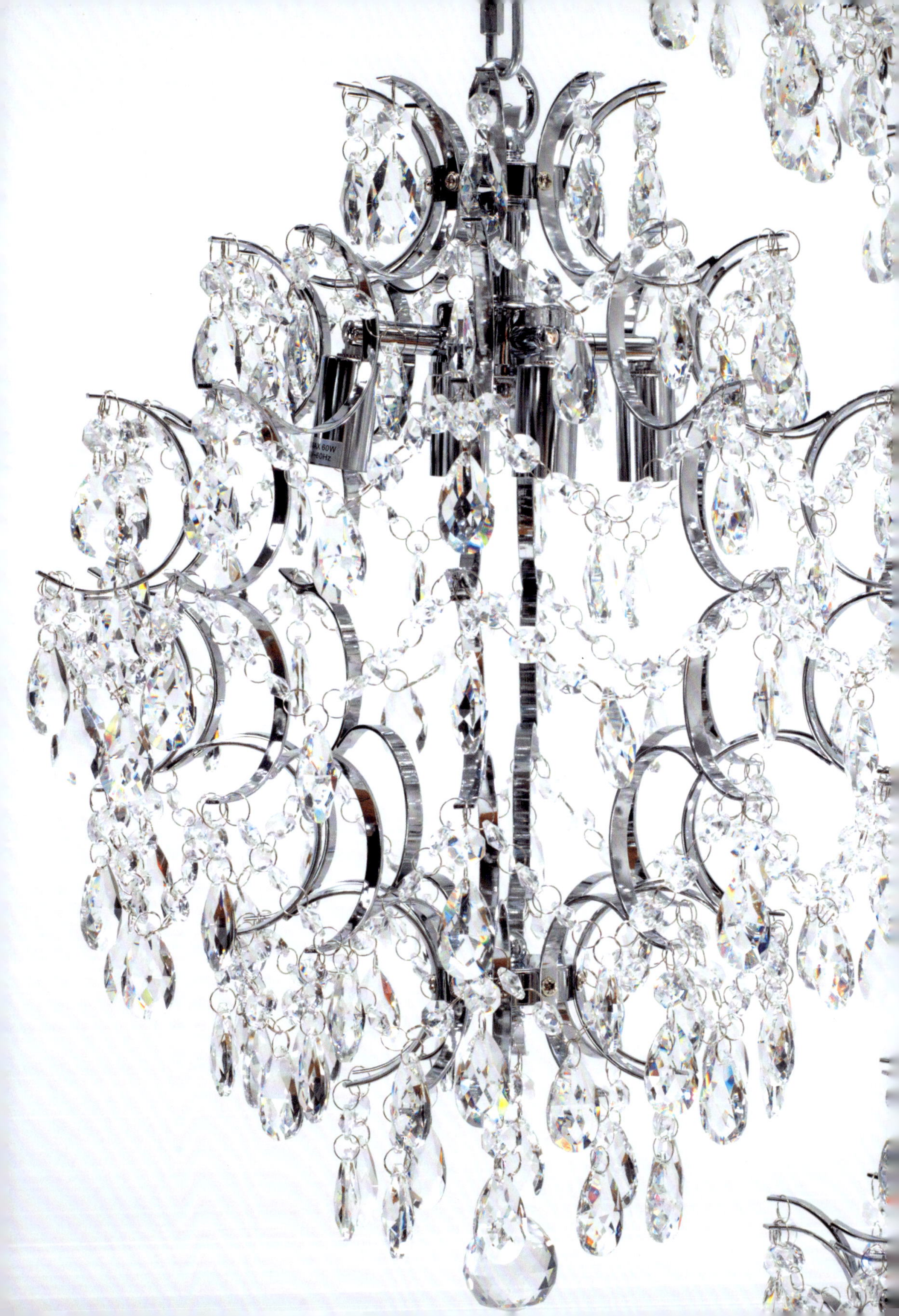

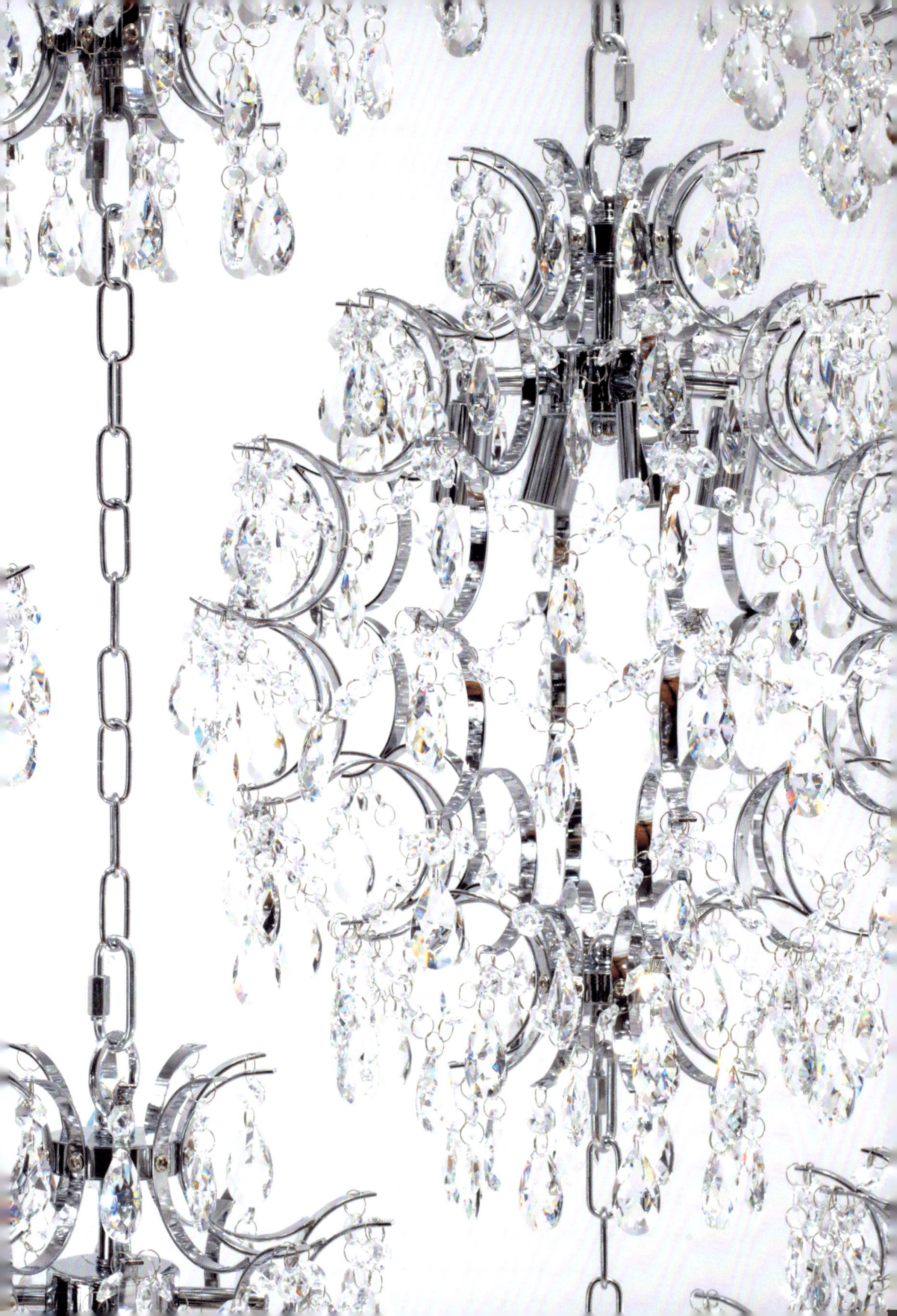

We thought it might go the other way, 2023
Eve Smoke Coupe Cocktail Glass; Glacier Bay Beveled
Edge Bath Mirror; Clear Amac Boxes; molar
35 ½ × 30 × 36 inches | 90.2 × 76.2 × 91.4 cm

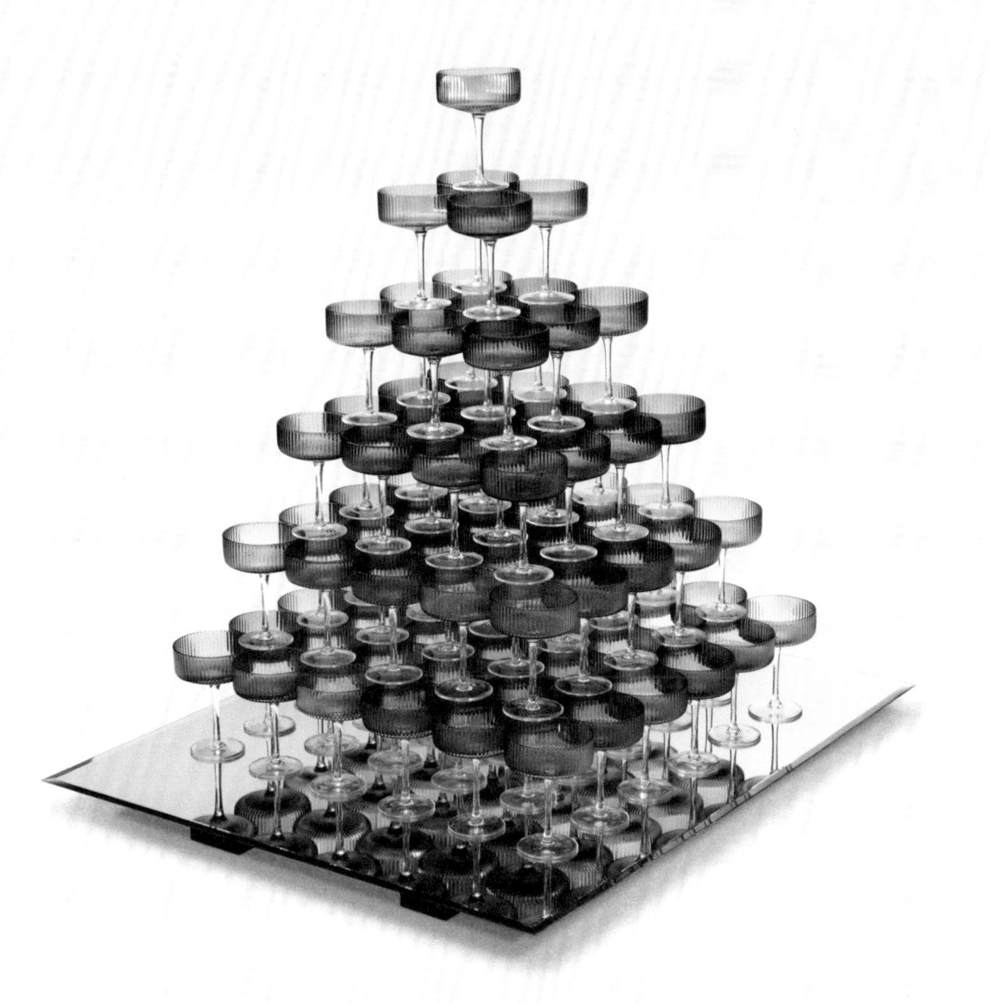

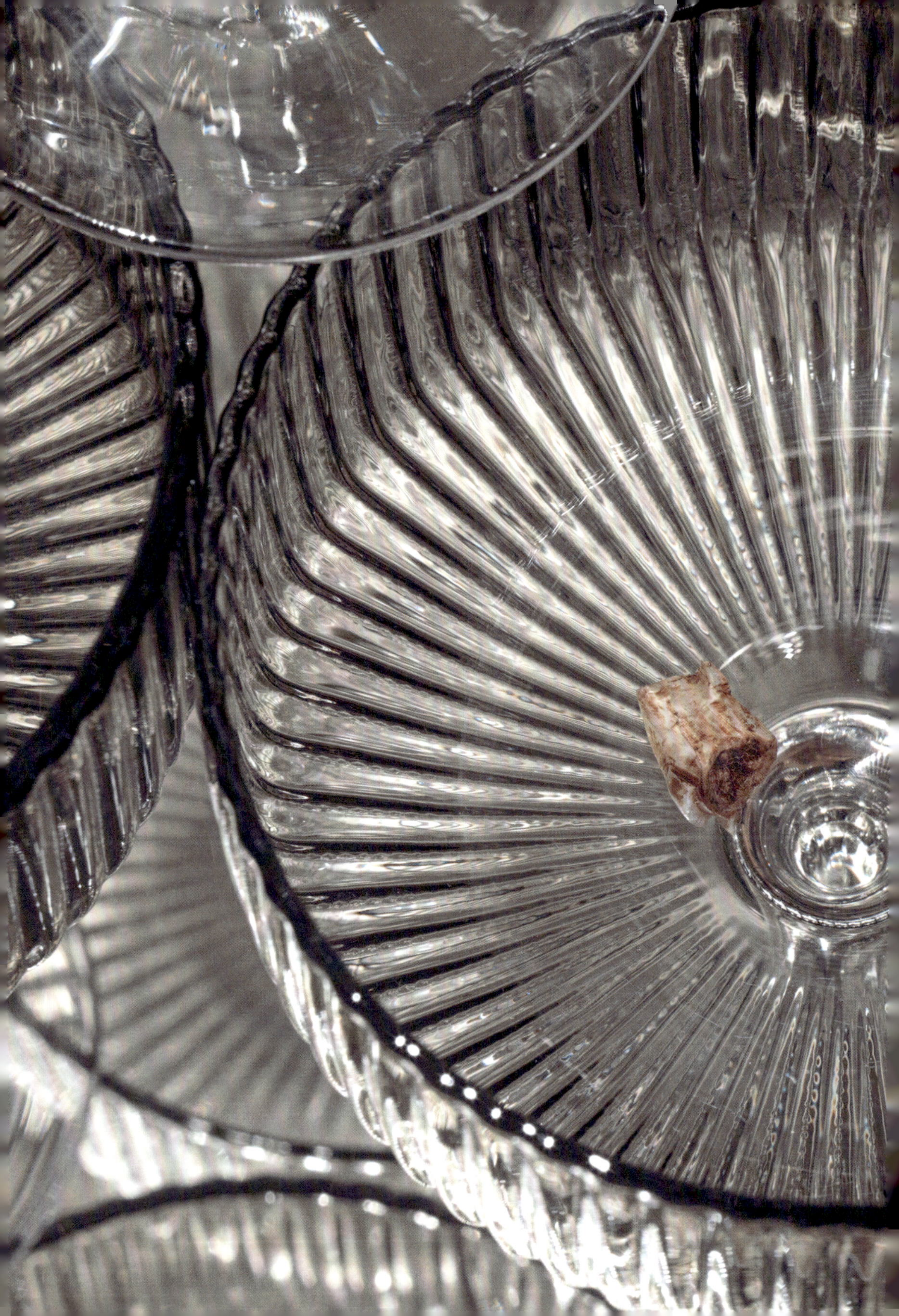

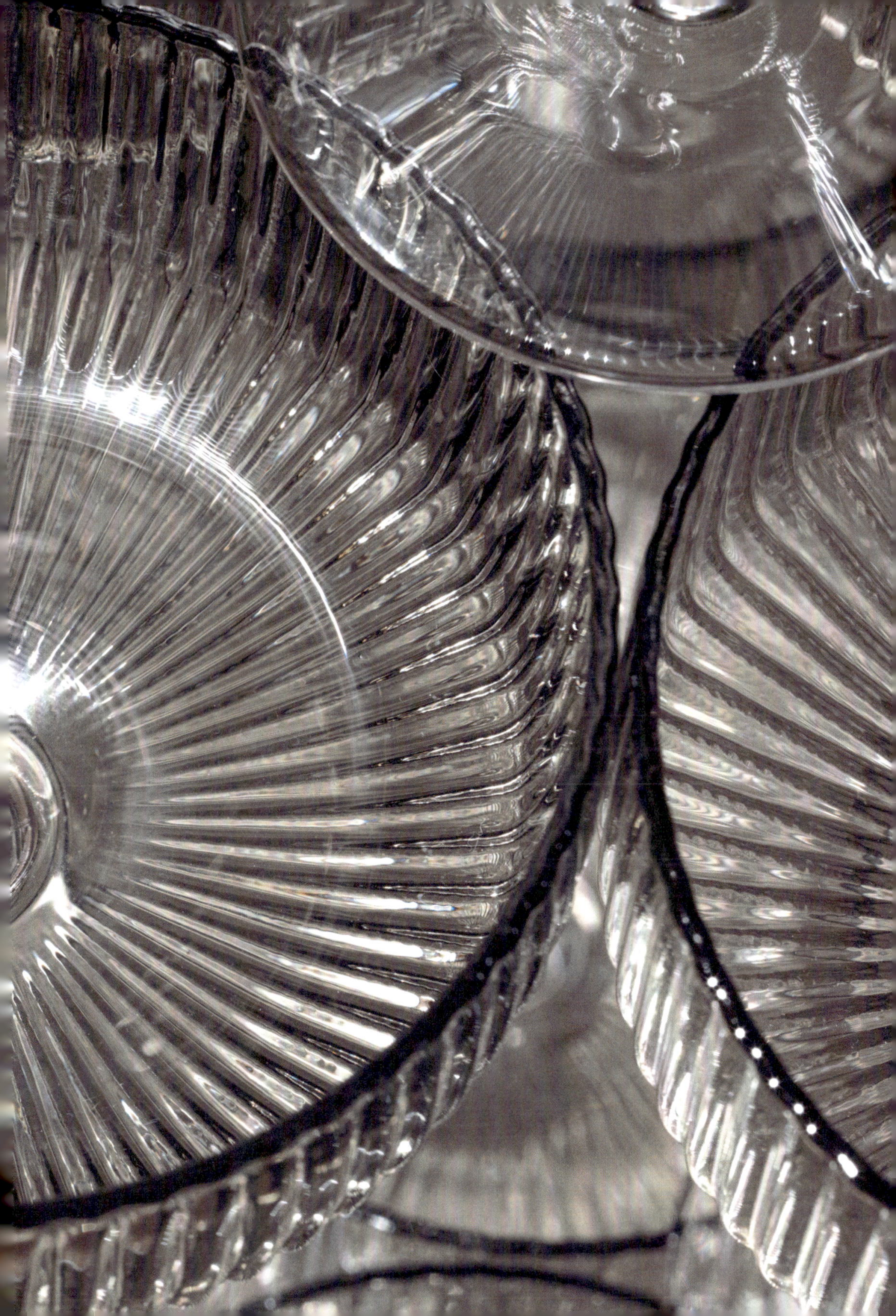

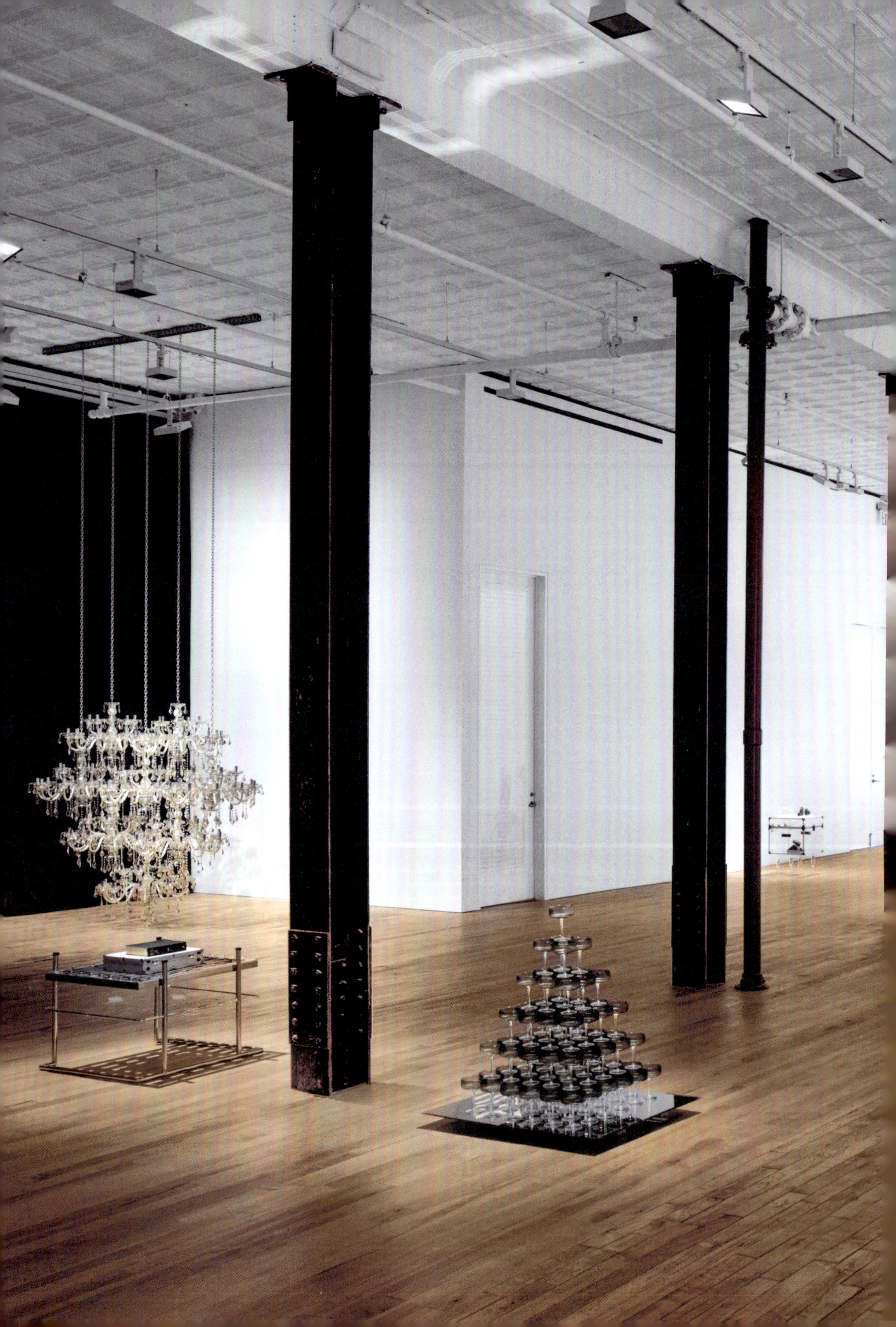

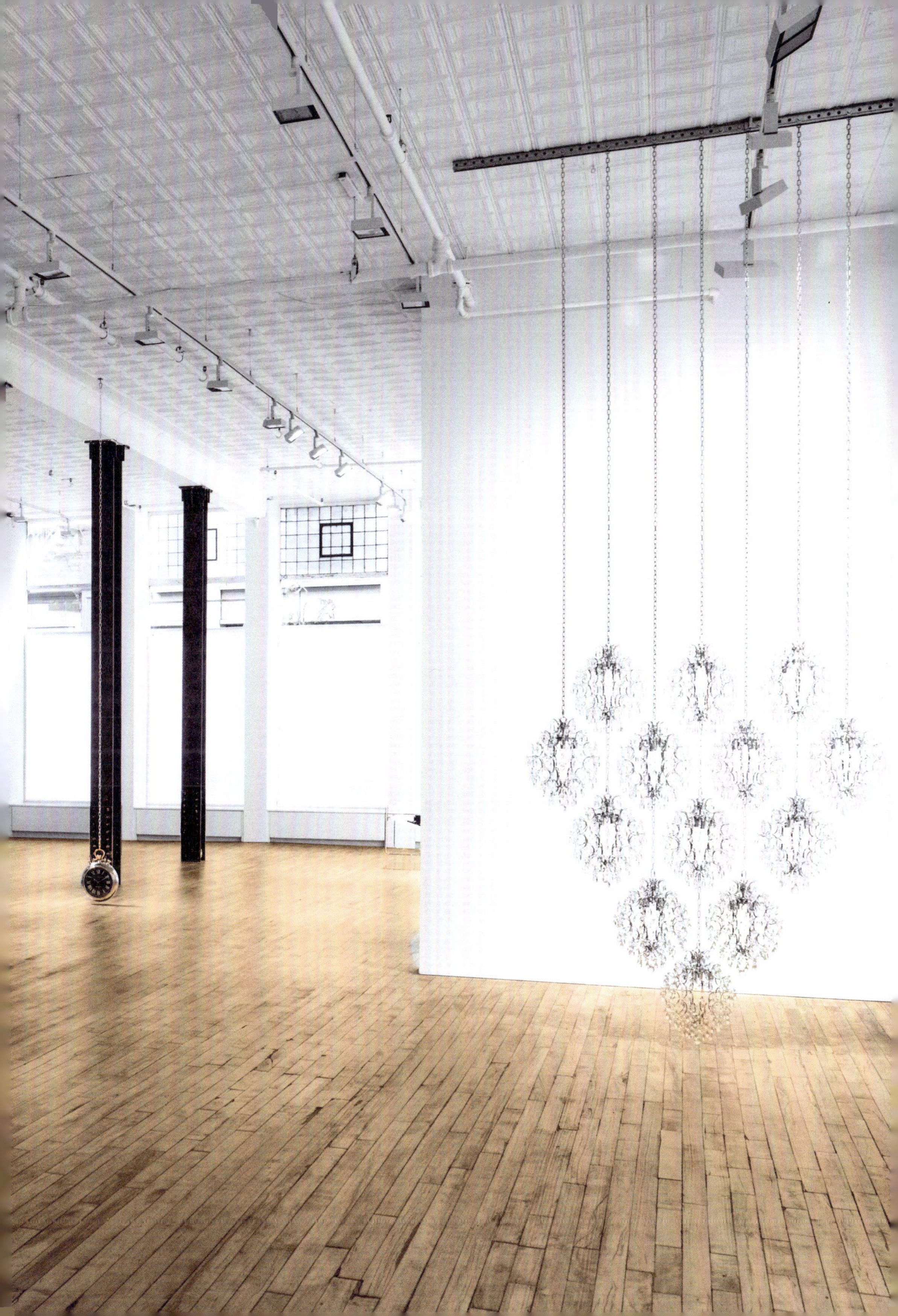

Dr. Land, 2023
Clear and Smoke Grey Acrylic Chess Set; Heavy Duty Toy Metal Handcuffs with Keys -
6 PACK Stainless Steel Bulk Fake Hand Cuffs Accessories Supplies for
Kids Police Pretend Role Play, Adult Party Favors; Mod Small Clear Acrylic Locker
Trunk; Polaroid SX-70 :: Original; Edge Champagne Glasses
30 ¼ × 18 ⅛ × 18 ¼ inches | 76.8 × 46 × 46.4 cm

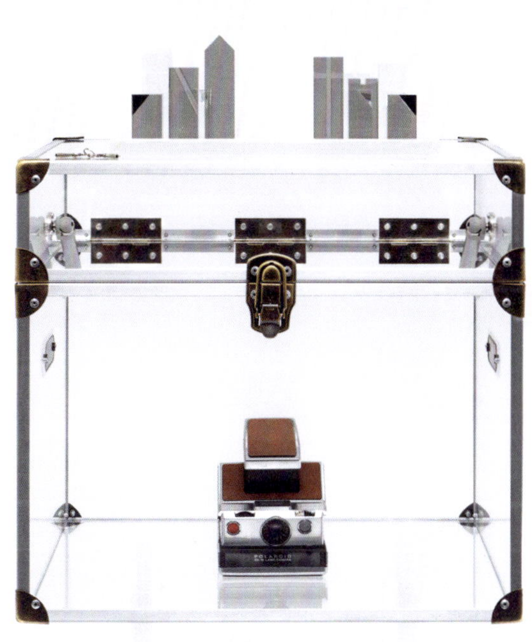

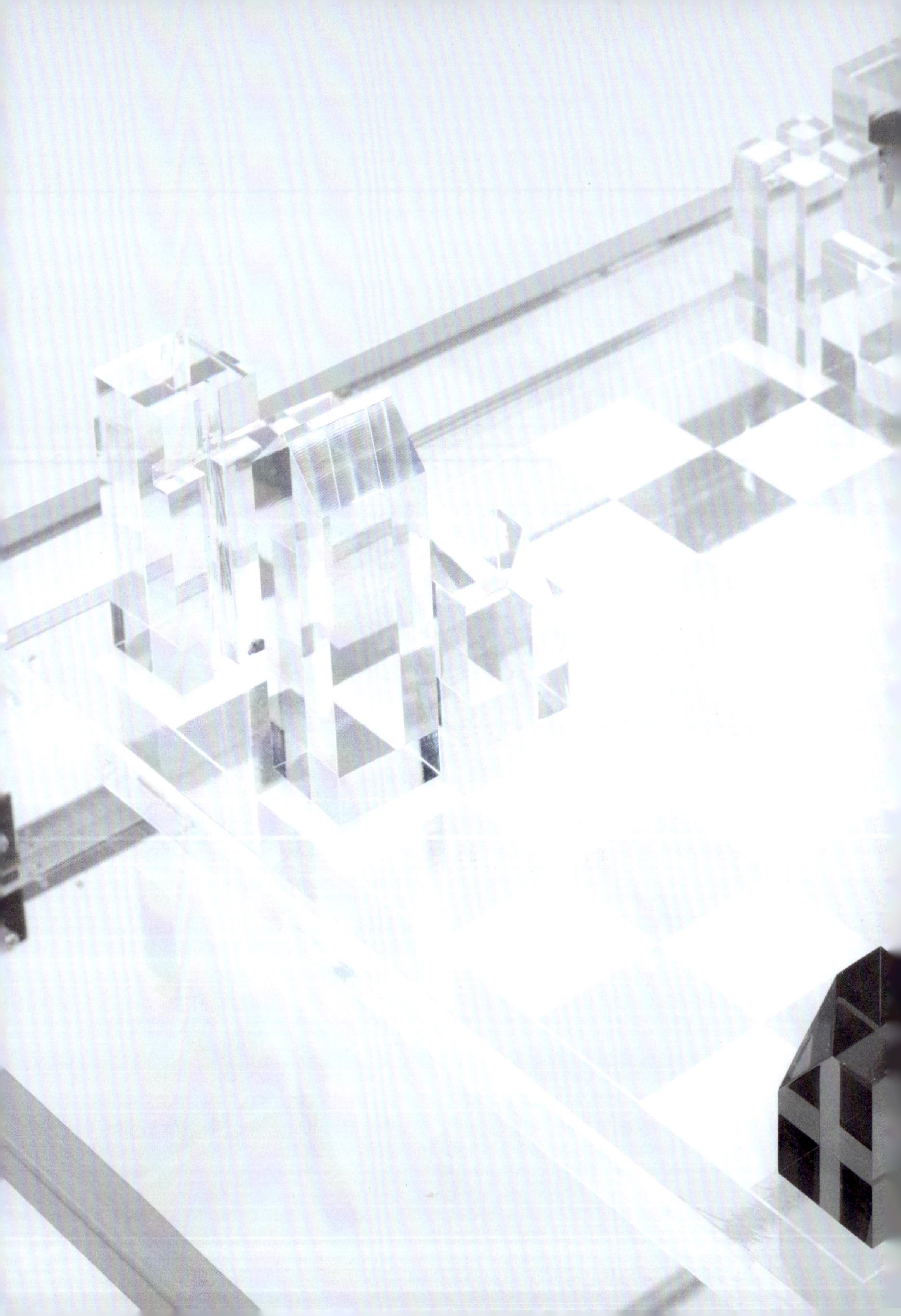

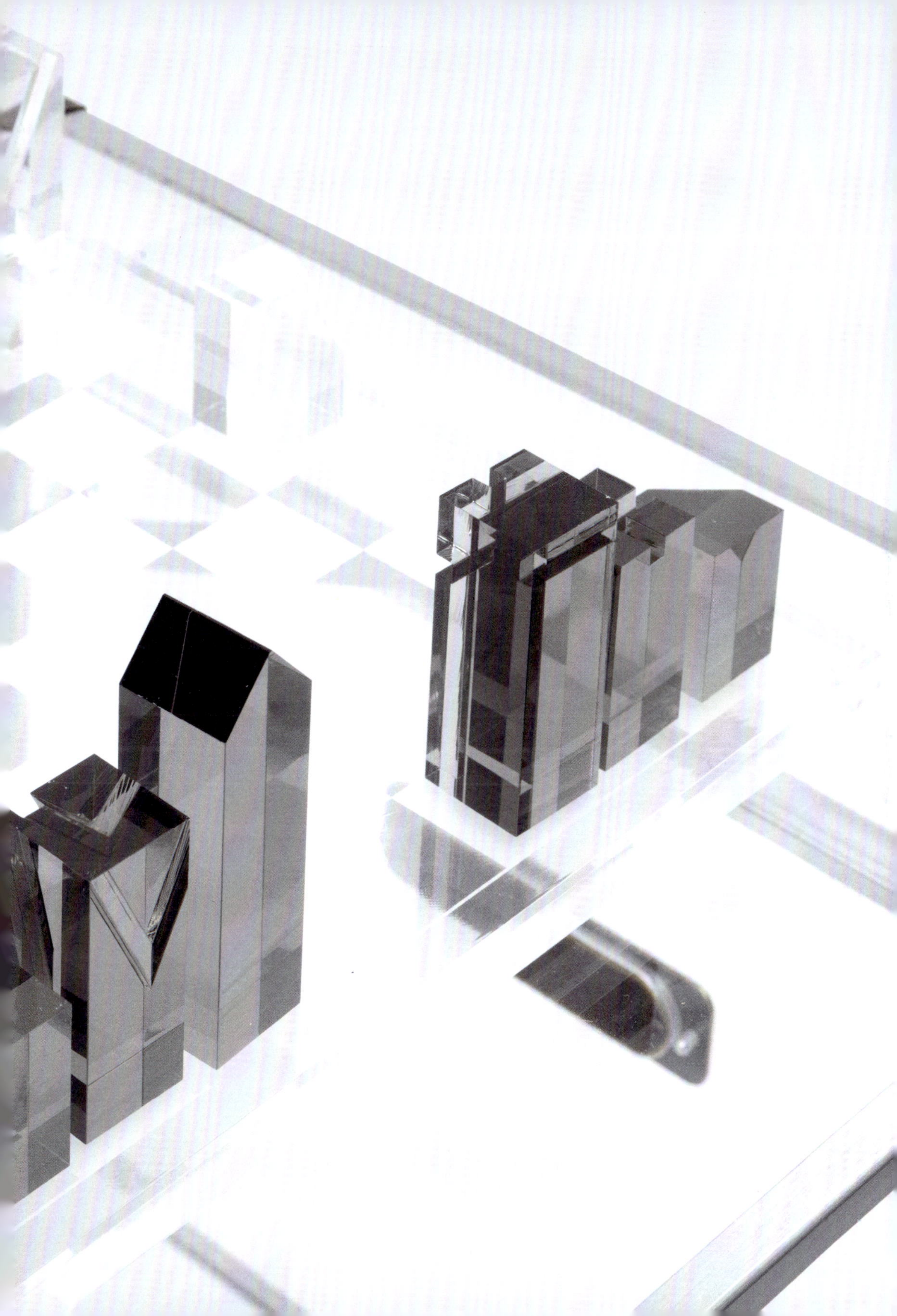

Basic Instinct, 2023
Graflex Speed Graphic Baby 2 1/4"x3 1/4" Camera w/ 101mm F4.5 Lens
Barely Used; Baxton Studio Jericho Leather Accent Chair – White; Clear
Amac Boxes; Glacier Bay Beveled Edge Bath Mirror
35 ¼ × 36 × 29 ⅞ inches | 89.5 × 91.4 × 75.9 cm

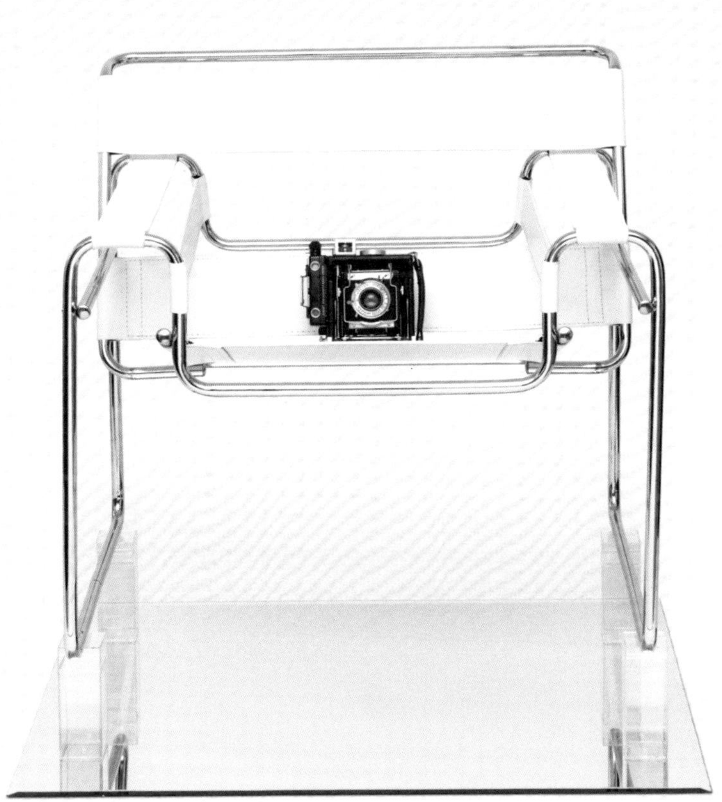

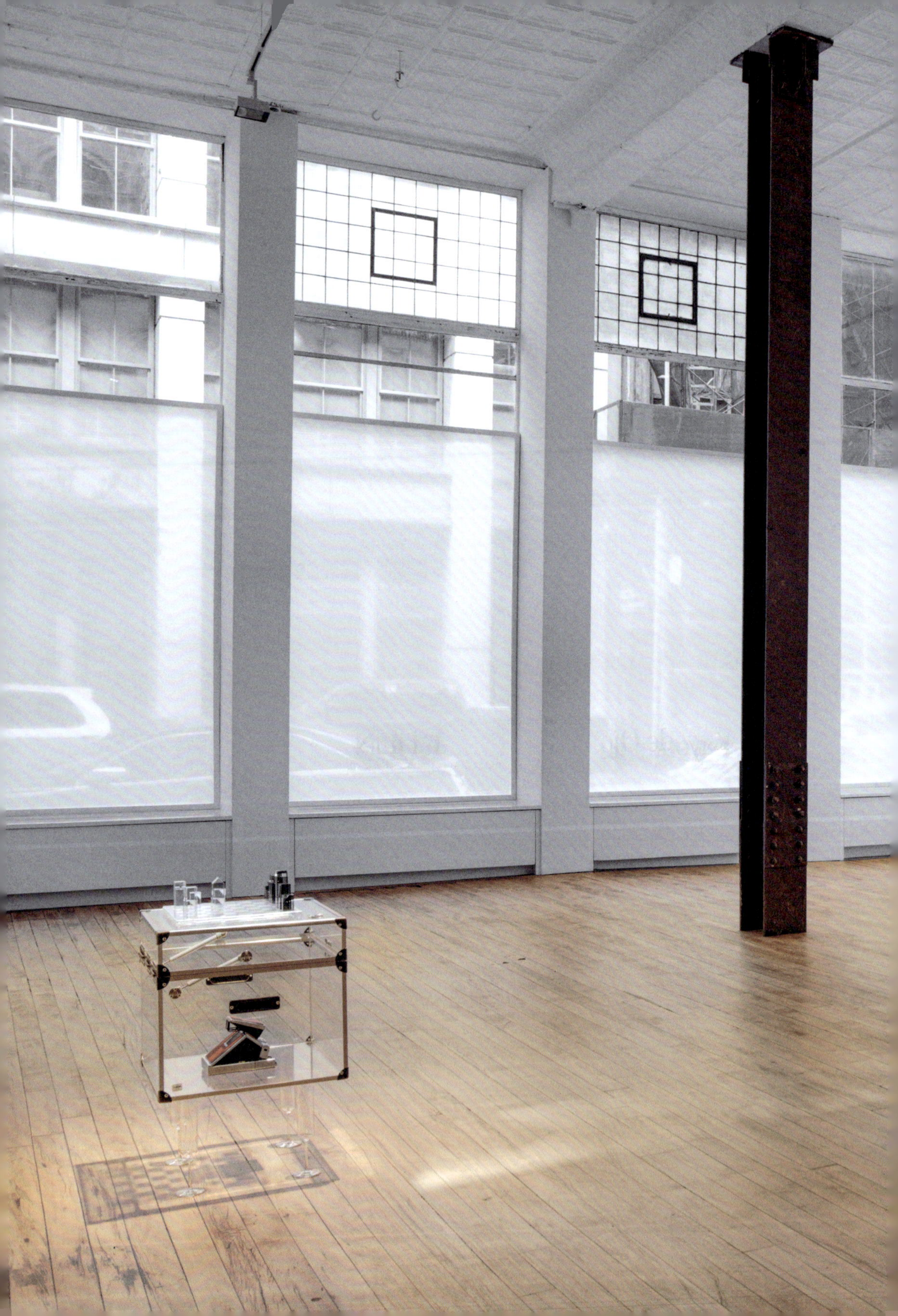

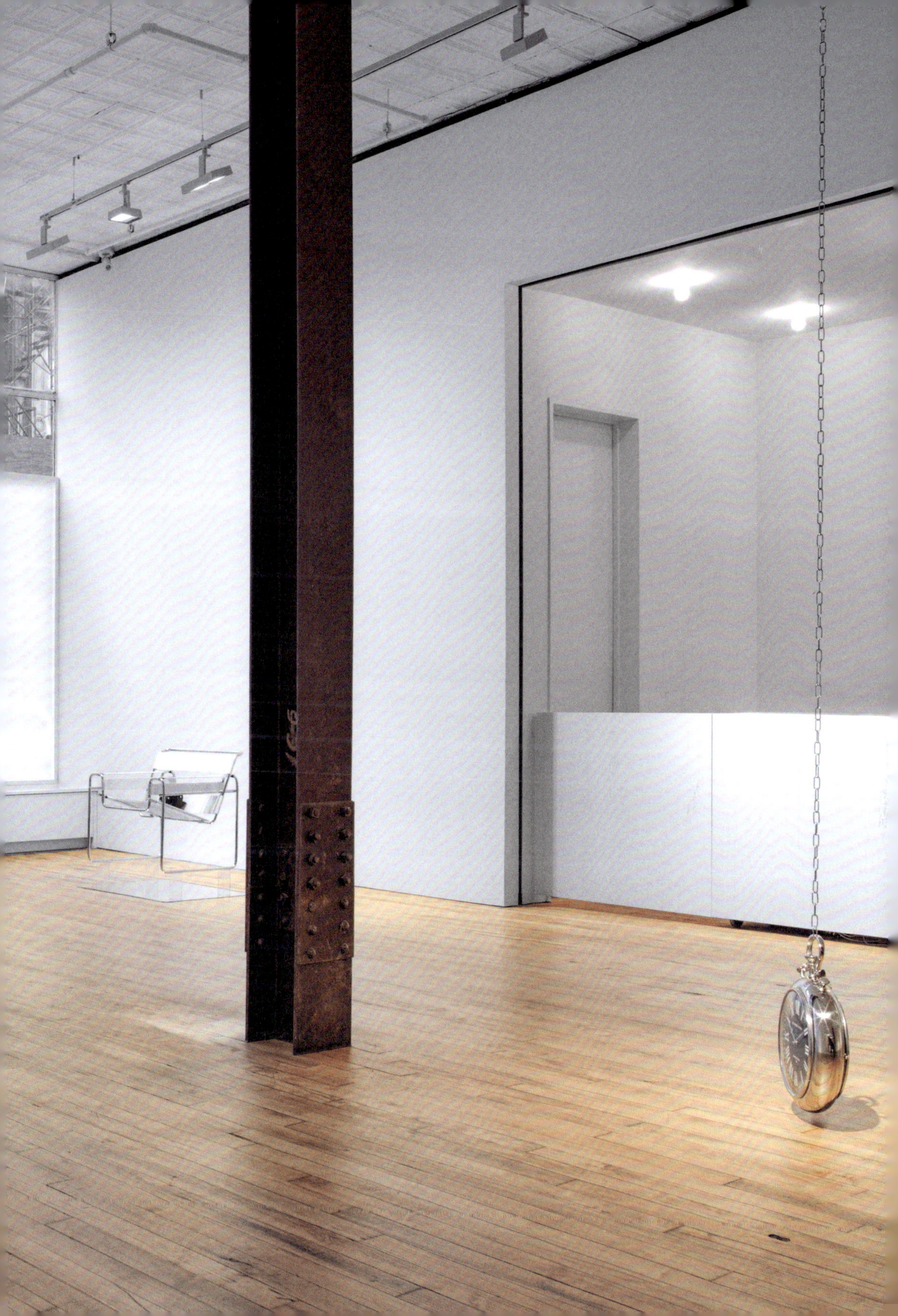

David Zwirner and Ebony L. Haynes wish to thank Kayode Ojo, without whom this exhibition and publication would not have been possible. Our thanks are also due to Serubiri Moses for his illuminating text.

For their work on the exhibition, we are grateful to Rebecca Ashby-Colón, Claire Ball, Cleo Bosmans, Susan Cernek, Jenny Cheng, Allison Chipak, Mark Espinosa, Karryl Eugene, Maris Hutchinson, Felice Jiang, Jordan Kelly, Coco Kim, Kevin Kramer, Gregory LaRico, Vida Lercari, Julia Lukacher, David McBride, Kerry McFate, Tessa Morefield, Jena Myung, Haley Darya Parsa, Julian Phillips, Erin Pinover, Nicholas Quint, Robert Richburg, Gabriela Scopazzi, Virginia Stroh, and Nora Woodin.

Thank you to Andrea Hyde for the catalogue series design and, for their work on this volume, to Bonnie Briant, Sergio Brunelli, Luke Chase, Fabio Ferrandini, Zeno Ferrandini, Doro Globus, Elizabeth Gordon, Jessica Palinski Hoos, Daniela Ioan, Avery Moore, Mari Perina, Chris Peterson, Molly Stein, Jules Thomson, Joey Young, and Lucas Zwirner.

The artist would like to thank Andrew Norman Wilson.

Collections

p. 21: Collection of Noel E. D. Kirnon
pp. 61, 79: Collection of Liv Barrett and Patrick Collins
p. 75: Didier Loulmet and Suzanne Butler Collection

Photography

p. 11: Courtesy Martos Gallery, New York. Photo by
Charles Benton
pp. 18–19, 21, 23, 24–25, 27, 29, 31, 33, 35, 36–37, 38–39,
41, 42–43, 45, 47, 48–49, 50–51, 53, 55, 57, 58–59, 61, 63, 65,
66–67, 69, 70–71, 72–73, 75, 76–77, 79, 80–81: Photos by
Kerry McFate

The *Clarion* series is an essential component of 52 Walker programming. An edition accompanies every exhibition, highlighting and expanding on the show's conceptual theses through newly commissioned texts, interviews, archival materials, and artistic interventions. The series is named in honor of the renowned author Octavia E. Butler, who was first published in the 1971 Clarion Science Fiction and Fantasy Writers' Workshop anthology.

Other Titles in the *Clarion* Series
I. Kandis Williams: A Line
II. Nikita Gale: END OF SUBJECT
III. Nora Turato: govern me harder
IV. Tiona Nekkia McClodden: MASK / CONCEAL / CARRY
V. Tau Lewis: Vox Populi, Vox Dei
VI. Gordon Matta-Clark & Pope.L: Impossible Failures
VII. Bob Thompson: So let us all be citizens
VIII. Heji Shin: THE BIG NUDES

Forthcoming Titles
X. Cauleen Smith: The Wanda Coleman Songbook
XI. Arthur Jafa: BLACK POWER TOOL AND
DIE TRYNIG

Published by 52 Walker and
David Zwirner Books
on the occasion of

Kayode Ojo: EDEN
52 Walker, New York
October 27, 2023–January 6, 2024

52 Walker
52 Walker Street
New York, New York 10013
+1 212 727 1961
52walker.com

David Zwirner Books
520 West 20th Street, 2nd Floor
New York, New York 10011
+1 212 727 2070
davidzwirnerbooks.com

Editor: Ebony L. Haynes
Project editor: Jessica Palinski Hoos
Proofreader: Chris Peterson

Clarion series design: Andrea Hyde
Layout: Bonnie Briant
Photography coordination: Rebecca Ashby-Colón,
    Virginia Stroh
Production manager: Luke Chase
Color separations: VeronaLibri, Verona
Printing: VeronaLibri, Verona

Typefaces: DTL Fleischmann, Genath
Paper: Magno Natural, 140 gsm

Publication © 2025 52 Walker and David Zwirner Books

"Curator's Note: Shine Bright like a Diamond"
    © 2025 Ebony L. Haynes
"Toward a Queer Postminimalism" © 2025 Serubiri Moses

All artwork by Kayode Ojo © 2025 Kayode Ojo

Distributed in the United States and Canada by
Simon & Schuster, Inc.
1230 Avenue of the Americas
New York, New York 10020
simonandschuster.com

Distributed outside the United States and Canada by
Thames & Hudson, Ltd.
181A High Holborn
London WC1V 7QX
thamesandhudson.com

ISBN 978-1-64423-156-2

Library of Congress Control Number: 2024942947

Printed in Italy

Notes

Notes

Notes